STUDIES OF THE INSTITUTE OF WORLD AFFAIRS

Management in Russian Industry and Agriculture

GREGORY BIENSTOCK, SOLOMON M. SCHWARZ,
and AARON YUGOW

. . .
.

EDITED BY
ARTHUR FEILER and JACOB MARSCHAK

OXFORD UNIVERSITY PRESS
LONDON NEW YORK TORONTO
1944

Second Printing, September, 1946

Printed in the United States of America

Preface

THIS study is a product of the Research Project on Social and Economic Controls in Germany and Russia, conducted by the Graduate Faculty of Political and Social Science of the New School for Social Research, with the support of the Rockefeller Foundation. It appears as the first volume in a series of international studies published under the auspices of the Institute of World Affairs, established by the New School for Social Research. It is perhaps superfluous to state that none of the sponsoring institutions identifies itself with the views expressed in this book. The research method applied excludes even a joint responsibility of the authors.

The work was instituted, and its scope delineated, by Arthur Feiler, whose death in the summer of 1942 deprived the collaborators of an invaluable guide and critic.

A debt of gratitude is due to Herbert Solow, who had the difficult task of translating part and editing all of the manuscript.

ADOLPH LOWE
Executive Director of Research

November 1943

Table of Contents

Authors of the different chapters are indicated by initials: B, *Gregory Bienstock;* S, *Solomon M. Schwarz;* Y, *Aaron Yugow.*

Note on Terminology and Citations

TRANSLITERATION in this book is according to the system used by the New York Public Library, with slight modifications.

For an understanding of Russian terms, it will be useful to consult the Glossary from time to time. General practice has been to use exact or approximate English equivalents, citing the Russian term on the first occasion. When it is impossible to render the meaning in English exactly or succinctly, we adhere to the Russian, dispensing with italics after the first use.

Some terms require special elucidation.

Plant: To denote the basic unit of industrial production in Russia, the State-owned and -controlled counterpart of the American 'firm' or 'concern,' the word 'plant' (occasionally 'factory,' 'mill,' 'shipyard,' etc.) is used. As far as possible, literal translation of *predpriyatiye*, enterprise, has been avoided; it is heavy, unfamiliar, and, with its connotations of the free and enterprising entrepreneur, misleading. 'Plant' is rather loose, colloquial, and non-committal, and has, on the whole, physical rather than social connotations. The reader will do well, however, to remember that the premises of what we call a plant may be widely scattered (e.g. a railroad). The term plant seems to work fairly well in a non-legal study.

Control: This word conveys in Russian (as in French and German) a much smaller degree of interference, domination, and authority than in English: it is best rendered, in the majority of cases, by 'supervision' or, less frequently, by 'inspection' or by 'comptrollership.' Throughout this book, control has been used in the broader English sense, as in 'one-man control' (*yedinonatchaliye;* see Glossary), except in the case of a specific Soviet slogan describing supervision of industry by State banks, i.e. 'Control by the Rouble' (Chapter VII).

Territorial Divisions: The Union of Soviet Socialist Republics consisted in 1940 of sixteen constituent Republics (*soyuznyye respubliki*—union Republics). Some include in their territory smaller units, in many respects autonomous, each inhabited by a compact national minority. These are the 'autonomous [national] Republics.' The less autonomous subdivisions of the constituent Republics we call 'provinces,' as a general equivalent of the official *oblast'*, the *krai* (certain outlying areas), the autonomous national oblast', and the somewhat smaller pre-revolutionary *guberniya.* For still smaller territorial units we use the general term 'district,' as an equivalent of *raion*, *okrug*, and (pre-revolutionary) *uyezd.* The administration of districts and of individual cities and villages we call *local*, reserving the term *regional* (and region) for higher administrative levels, i.e. provinces, autonomous Republics, and constituent Republics.

Congresses of the Communist Party of the Soviet Union, the supreme Party organ, represent Party members directly and are, according to Party statutes, supposed to convene triennially. All-Union Party *conferences* are supposed to convene not less than annually in intervals between Congresses to discuss urgent Party problems. Conference delegates are elected not by Party members but by the Party's regional, provincial, and Republic committees.

The Congresses chiefly referred to in this book are as follows:

8th: March 1919
9th: March-April 1920
10th: March 1921
11th: March-April 1922
12th: April 1923
13th: May 1924
14th: December 1925
15th: December 1927
16th: June-July 1930
17th: January-February 1934
18th: March 1939

Capital letters are used in this book somewhat more generally than is standard English language practice. The deviation aims at assisting the reader to bear constantly in mind certain special connotations which, in any discussion of the Soviet regime, should attach to commonplace words.

Thus, the words *Party* and *State*, whenever they apply to the Communist Party or the Soviet State, are capitalized in order to emphasize that in the U.S.S.R. the relation of these institutions to economic life is fundamentally different from any comparable relationship in Great Britain or the United States. Soviet economic life is ruled by the Soviet State, the Soviet State in turn by the Communist Party of the Soviet Union.

Likewise, the word *Plan* has been capitalized whenever the reference is to the overall national Plan. The object is to distinguish sharply this comprehensive instrument, something quite alien to Western experience, from plans familiar to the Westerner but far more limited geographically, technically, or otherwise. There have been three such overall Plans, each of five years' duration. The period of the first was to have been from 1 October 1928 to 30 September 1933; it was declared finished on 31 December 1932. The next two periods were 1933-7 and 1938-42, both inclusive.

Titles of Russian books are quoted in English translation, as are titles of newspapers and magazines, except when their Russian names are well known. Titles of articles are given only in cases of large magazines, and only in English. For magazines, bulletins, and newspapers, the Russian titles are presented at the end of the book, under the heading *Titles of Russian Periodicals*, in a list alphabetized according to the English translation.

Laws and Ordinances: Official Soviet collection, *Sobraniye Zakonov i Rasporyazhenii Pravitel'stva Soyuza Sotzialisticheskikh Sovietskikh Respublik* (after 1938, *Sobraniye Postanovlenii i Rasporyazhenii*, etc.). Cited with reference to the year and current number of the law or ordinance. For example, *Laws and Ordinances*, 1938:286.

Party Congress: Official stenographic reports of Congresses of the Communist Party of the U.S.S.R. For example, 18th Party Congress, p. 654.

Decisions: Decisions of Communist Party organs. Cited from the official collection, *Vsesoyuznaya Kommunisticheskaya Partiya v Rezolyutziyakh S'yezdov, Konferentzii i Plenumov Tzentral'nogo Komiteta* (The Communist Party of the U.S.S.R. in Resolutions of Party Congresses, Conferences and Plenary Sessions of the Central Committee), 6th edition, 2 vols. (Moscow, 1940). For example, *Decisions*, 1:452.

Introduction

BY JACOB MARSCHAK

TO study Russia today is to measure the strength of an all-important factor in war and peace. To take this measure is also to contribute to the age-old discussion whether, at what tasks, and under what circumstances, honor-seeking officials are more or less efficient than profit-seeking businessmen; whether and when fear of degradation and punishment is a more or less powerful deterrent than fear of financial loss; to what extent economic initiative may be effectively centralized or decentralized. These are questions limited by no geographical boundaries.

Several excellent studies have tried to give answers by describing and measuring the final aggregate effect of the Russian system, and the success or failure of the Five Year Plans and collectivized farming as a whole; in addition, we may now expect analyses of Russian military defeats and victories as so many tremendous, if incomplete, tests of the Soviet economic and social system.

The present book has a different emphasis. Its focus is not on aggregate results that the huge machinery has produced or has failed to produce, but on some of the smallest constituent units of economic volition—the single industrial plant, the single collective farm. More particularly, it centers on the managers of plants, the chairmen and other officers of collective farms (*kolkhozes*).

Technological data, laws of physics and chemistry, are the same for the Soviet plant manager and his equivalent in America. Differences arising from geographical position, size, or natural resources are not too formidable. Differences in human material, although enormous, are probably diminishing, in so far as learned industrial skill is concerned. It is the institutions, the man-made laws and practices, which make managerial activities in Russian industry and agriculture so different from those of this country.

Nowhere do the peculiarities of total planning and collective farming under the all-decisive rule of Party-State reveal themselves more strikingly than in the functions and incentives of Russian plant and kolkhoz administrators. On the other hand, in no field can one learn more from the similarities—actual or emergent or re-emergent—between Soviet economic institutions and the administrative or economic practices of other countries, especially under war pressure. To the student of human organization, both are instructive: that which varies and that which persists, the peculiar and the common.

Millions of people are in combat; farms and cities, factories, mines, shipyards, have been lost to the enemy or have become battlefields. Can one describe 'management in industry and agriculture' where both are truncated? The complicated machinery of long-term planning, of directing and supervising, must have lost much of its subtle detail: war's daily needs are too brutal, communications and government are strained or torn into parts. Production continues amidst scarcity and ruin. And management often means maintaining work just behind the front, or precariously evacuating and reintegrating salvage.

But Russian economic institutions in war are not the subject of this book. For such a study, reliable material is not yet at hand. Except occasionally, the authors have not tried to go beyond 22 June 1941, the day of the German invasion. Their present tense is the historical present.

Nevertheless, the conditions they analyze have more than 'merely historical' value, to use an expression popular with those who think that history is only for the historians. We do not think so. There is no doubt, to be sure, that such a war as the present greatly affects both men and their laws. It would be folly to exclude the possibility of profound economic changes and political shifts, and a consequent resetting of Russian economic institutions after the war. Yet, without claiming that 1941 equals 1945, the authors have found in the material of pre-1941 much that will be useful for an understanding of 1945, of 1950, perhaps even of a more remote future.

Leaving post-war Russia aside, its pre-war experiments are instructive in themselves. The American reader will often recognize administrative puzzles and struggles of our own centralized war economy. He may welcome the test of certain principles carried to their extreme.

As in so many fields where interest and belief prevail over the quest for truth, debates on Russia, in both word and print, have often been at cross-purposes. Worse still, labels have often been substituted for facts:

'Nazism and Communism are really the same thing.'

'Nazism and Communism are opposite philosophies.'

'The Soviet system is socialism and therefore bad.'

'The Soviet system is socialism and therefore good.'

'The Soviet system is a caricature of socialism.'

'What is socialism?'

The discussion begins turning hopelessly on abstract concepts, ill-defined, emotionally overloaded, whether called socialism or technocracy or state capitalism or managerial revolution. Of course, there are many countries with certain ascertainable common features to which one can reasonably agree to give a common name, say, capitalism. But why quarrel whether an animal species of which only one individual has ever been observed (and that one imperfectly) is a snark or a jubjub?

In assigning to a research group the task of analyzing management in Russian industry and agriculture, the Graduate Faculty asked them to ascertain facts, not discuss words. A picture was to be drawn, as detailed as the data would permit, of the machinery of Soviet management; of the distribution of functions and powers in factory and farm; of the origin, status, incentives, and, if possible, ideology of managerial personnel.

Reserve and caution in reaching conclusions were obviously essential. Where appraisal was made, such criteria were applied as are generally recognized in discussions of economic and social policy. Contribution to higher national income by producing larger quantities of better and more useful goods was considered a success, the opposite, a failure. More participation of individuals in the shaping of their work and life was considered a positive value: hence the concern with the role of labor unions, with the self-government of kolkhozes, and with inequalities in social status and power.

Yet any such evaluation had to remain incomplete: a study on management can cover but a corner of the whole problem of the productivity, equality, liberty of the people engaged in Russia's production. Nor was any attempt made to praise or blame the government for the way in which shares of product have been apportioned among consumption, investment, and armament. Furthermore, as few data are available on the operation of plants producing finished war equipment, most information given in the study is confined to raw materials and semi-finished goods (including metals and fuel) and to civilian consumption goods.

Students of capitalism are wont to see in the entrepreneur's profit the mainspring of economic action. He is spurred to expand or innovate by hope of gain, deterred from producing by fear of loss. He uses his money, or that entrusted to him by stockholders or lenders, to employ labor, machines, materials, in those industries and in such ways as promise the highest profits. His judgment and that of his competitors, if such there be, therefore determine how a country's resources are used.

A line has been drawn, to be sure, between 'entrepreneurial' decisions thus defined and the activities of the 'manager' pure and simple, doing routine work and obtaining as his reward a more or less fixed salary rather than an uncertain profit. But the distinction is not easy when expanding output, changing techniques, and fluctuating markets make routine management exceptional. In fact, there is probably a large body of people, including those at the head of large corporate enterprises, who are at once entrepreneurs and managers (although not always 'capitalists,' i.e. suppliers of capital). These are the 'businessmen.'

Soviet industry is managed, from top to bottom, by salaried officials. Their income is but loosely connected with profits of the plants or groups of plants they manage: it will be seen that the connection is much more remote than in the case of corporation officials. One might be inclined to seek analogies in the major well-established State-run enterprises of capitalist countries: the United States Post Office, European State railroads, State credit institutions. One might thus conceive of Russian industry as run by 'pure managers' in government pay. But Russian economic life of this generation cannot, by any stretch of the imagination, be called routine: the country's industry has rapidly expanded, its agriculture has been reorganized, new methods have been adopted with enthusiasm, plans of revolutionary scope are made and constantly revised.

To be sure, Soviet law and literature try to distinguish current 'operative' functions—procuring and disposing of goods, hiring labor, supervising production—from 'planning' proper, and, more generally, from 'directives' or policy-making. In theory, the manager of a single plant is confined to operative functions, while special government organs do the planning, within general directives provided by the Party. It will be seen that this theory is neither comprehensive, nor final, nor applied. It leaves ill-defined the functions of powerful administrative organs; it is being constantly modified and occasionally reversed; it is often contradicted in practice.

Who, then, makes decisions and shoulders responsibilities corresponding to those of an American businessman? Not the head of a single plant or collective farm. Perhaps, then, Stalin in person? If neither is fully the case, how is responsibility shared between top government departments in Moscow, intermediate organs for areas or industries, and, say, a plant manager? How are all these bodies and persons related to those who write the Five Year Plans and to State banks which dispense credit? With the Communist Party in absolute control of government, and with regional and, to some extent, functional ramifications of the Party paralleling those of the State, how much can the State official say and the Party official unsay? To whom does the plant manager or kolkhoz chairman owe ultimate allegiance? In particular, what has been the power of Party members who happen to be employees of a plant? Or of village Communists, local or imported, whose business it has been to speed collectivization? How much self-government or co-partnership or labor-union influence is there in the working community of a Russian industrial plant? How strong, in collectively run farms, are elements of co-operative production as compared with elements of State control or with those residuals of individualist farming, the homestead plots?

Under Soviet conditions of economy, functions pertaining to management have acquired highly characteristic forms. The peculiarities of the day-to-day tasks of a single Soviet-manager are probably less known to the American reader than is the general idea of total centralized planning. Those tasks are profoundly affected by the Plan (whether fulfilled or not) and by the almost complete absence of free markets. How does the manager obtain liquid funds, raw materials, and machine parts? How does he supply others with his products? How were the vast human masses recruited, to build and run new gigantic factories? Who fixes their wages and working conditions? The peculiarities of current farm management are, if possible, even greater: kolkhozes are a novel production form.

Both the quantities and prices of industrial goods are fixed by authorities. The manager, head of the lowest unit of industrial administration, participates in the working out of details, not of general outlines of a Five Year Plan or its currently revised short-term versions. And, although over-fulfilment of the allotted quota is encouraged and rewarded, production of a plant must, on the whole, appear rigid as compared with the extremely flexible output of a capitalist enterprise, sensitive to minute changes in profit expectation. The plant's capacity is fixed by outside authorities. In theory, at least, construction funds at the manager's disposal are limited to repairs and, under certain conditions, to workers' housing construction. To sell parts of a plant or equipment is strictly illegal. The most important materials are allocated from above. True, many of these procedures and limitations have remained on paper, have been evaded or breached in practice. It has been the attempt of the authors to study both theory and practice.

The Soviet manager is unable to manipulate freely the size of his plant or his inventories. Nor can he take advantage of market situations, current or prospective, by bargaining with sources of supplies or with customers for better prices, or by winning customers through low prices, and sources of supplies through high ones. To be sure, with supply chronically lagging behind demand, it would in any case be pointless for a manager to reduce prices in order to win customers. On the other hand, to win preference from a source of supplies by bidding up prices for raw materials would not be pointless.—But it is forbidden.

The fixing of price and output is a logical feature of overall planning. One possible avenue of escape from fixed prices and prescribed production figures is by making inferior goods. The government naturally—if not always successfully—tries to block this escape.

The manager's energies are thus directed into the one remaining channel: reduction of real unit costs of production, i.e. the amount of materials and labor going into one unit of product. A fixed portion of the fixed factory price is called 'planned profit,' the other portion 'planned costs.' But a skillful manager, worthy of honors, promotions, and bonuses, is expected to bring actual costs below planned costs and thus to raise profits above the planned figure. On the other hand, to let actual cost rise above planned cost is to fall short of planned profits or even—if costs reach fixed price—to incur loss: such a manager is frowned upon, investigated—perhaps demoted, transferred, or punished—unless he can show that prices of raw materials and labor had risen (thus affecting money cost, not real cost), or unless the plant is working under government subsidy.

Subsidies, formerly the rule, had by 1940 become exceptions. The rediscovery of the profit principle was hailed as an achievement crowning the gradual return of industry to business accountability, so completely abandoned in the early years of revolution, during War Communism and hyper-inflation.

Yet Soviet plant profit is very different from its Western counterpart. As we have just seen, a Soviet manager can make or miss profit only by his success or failure in keeping unit costs down. But whether or not profits rise, they have only a very indirect connection with the income of the manager, his supervisors, planning officials, or whoever may be regarded as the Russian counterpart of the American businessman. The beneficiaries of any profits made by the plant are the State, the capital reserves of the plant, and certain special funds designed to foster welfare and efficiency of personnel. Bonuses to managers are calculated on the basis not of profits but of extra output or achieved cost reduction. Profits are only one of the dozen arithmetically interdependent indices of success that plant accountants and statisticians must work out for the current information of higher agencies of State industry.

One might, therefore, ask why profit, being merely the difference between government-fixed prices multiplied by government-fixed output, and the costs of production, should be given so much attention by Soviet economists as a particularly important success-indicator, a new and efficient weapon of planned economy. Since the profit figure provides no information concerning the success of the plant not already contained in cost and output figures, and since all these figures are reported to higher authorities (who periodically mete out blame or praise), why does Soviet literature single out profits as a particular 'incentive,' somewhat reminiscent of the private entrepreneurial profits of capitalist countries?

The truth is that even under capitalism the entrepreneur's profit does more than add to his income. It also enlarges his radius of influence; in particular, the entrepreneur is able to use a part of profits to enlarge the plant entrusted to him. But so is the Soviet manager, at least in so far as the portion of profits allotted to the plant's capital fund is concerned. In addition, the special welfare and efficiency funds entrusted to the manager raise his influence and prestige with the personnel.

Overall planning is thus combined with a rather mild dose of profit incentive. But profits can be made only by reducing costs. Since prices are fixed, cost economies are not passed on to consumers but are divided between the State and the plant.

This is similar to what happens under capitalism to cost economies in a monopolistic enterprise subject to corporation tax. The consumer benefits from technical progress not fully and surely, as he would if free competition were to bring the price down to the new cost level and thus release a part of the consumer's income to be spent as he chooses; here he benefits only in part and uncertainly. A portion of profits arising from cost economies remains in the successful plant. It is very likely used to expand output, even though the public may not be eager to increase exclusively its consumption of the products of that particular plant or industry. Another portion of the profit goes to finance State expenditures. By a happy accident, the State may invest its receipts so as to make exactly those goods or services most eagerly sought by the public. But this is not necessarily the case. By withholding cost economies from consumers, the system deprives them of the possibility of influencing the allocation of labor and other resources released by technical progress.

True, decisions about expenditures on, say, army and armaments (or even schools and pavements) cannot be made dependent on each single man in the market and his desire to save or consume certain goods and services rather than others. Taxation is inevitable for such purposes. If, furthermore, the considered policy of the State is to expand the country's equipment rapidly, it may be impossible to rely on the individual's desire to save. In other words, the public representatives or officials may consider themselves, in these particular fields, less indolent and shortsighted than their constituents or subjects, more apt to see and provide for the common good if not of this, then of the next generation. Thus in every economic system arises the question how to provide for army, schools, possibly for expansion of industry, while using the remainder of national resources to the best satisfaction of consumer desires.

The Russian answer has been an enormous turnover tax. In addition, since prices and outputs are fixed, the State's fixed share in profits (especially in their 'planned' part, i.e. apart from cost economies) differs only in form from the turnover tax. Together, the turnover tax and the State's profit share are so large as to destroy all relation between cost to consumer and cost to producer. The comparative urgency which buyers assign to various goods has no effect on prices they must pay, since they cannot bid up prices or force them down.

The Russian schedule of fixed prices, as well as of variegated sales-tax rates, suggests that the ruling principle has been that of all monopolists, to charge 'what the traffic will bear,' with high taxes and profit margins for articles of urgent consumer need. Were State revenues of equal amount collected by income tax, and managers compelled to sell at cost[1] (including managerial

[1] Here cost means marginal cost (i.e. the cost of making an additional unit of output), not average cost (i.e. all the past or current outlays of the producer divided by the output they have helped to create). It is essential that the cost of hiring additional workers or of adding new equipment to satisfy consumer demand influences price and output, thus directing men and equipment to the uses most wanted. On the other hand, price and output must not be influenced, for example, by depreciation charges on such old equipment as will not be replaced and as would not have been installed had

salaries as well as other wages), the consumer-workers would arrange their budgets (after tax) as best they liked, bidding up prices of the most desired goods, thus raising wages payable in the most urgently needed industries, and offering their labor in those very industries. National resources, apart from those earmarked for specific State functions, would thus be used in the way most desired by the individuals.

This is true of a progressive as well as of a flat income tax, pro-

present techniques and tastes been foreseen. This point of view has been developed, with respect to any enterprise run in the public interest, by Dickinson, Hall, Hotelling, Lange, Lerner, Meade, Pigou, and others. The distinction is important and must not be waved aside by such remarks—true but irrelevant—as 'in the long run, average and marginal cost are identical' and 'under free competition, price is equal to marginal cost but also, in the long run, to average cost.' Practical decisions are made in the short, not the long run. The mechanism of free competition attracting or repelling private producers by profits or losses in individual industries does tend to annihilate any excess of price (and hence of marginal costs) over average costs, or vice versa. But this mechanism cannot and need not be copied in the case of managers of public plants. Their prescribed duty need not be to raise profit, but can, instead, require them to arrange production so as to equate the cost of making a new unit with its market price. There is no reason why construction of new public equipment should be financed out of revenue earned on old and outdated public equipment rather than out of general public funds raised by taxation of incomes.

The character of the present introduction precludes more thorough discussion of this point. It was not possible to provide in the relevant chapter (VI) sufficient material on the depreciation policy of Soviet price-fixers and accountants. This is partly because of lacunae in the Russian legal and economic sources. Soviet legislators and writers pay little regard to this point. They have taken over wholesale the traditional accountancy principles of private firms (such as the Lancashire cotton mill run by Friedrich Engels), as correctly seen and described by Karl Marx. Put in the position of running public-owned industry, Soviet economists have uncritically transferred from the private to the public sphere both a respect for profits and a suspicion of subsidies.

In this connection, see H. D. Dickinson, *Economics of Socialism* (Oxford, 1939), especially Ch. III; R. L. Hall, *The Economic System in a Socialist State* (London, 1937); Harold Hotelling, 'The General Welfare in Relation to Problems of Taxation and of Railway and Utility Rates,' in *Econometrica*, VI:3 (July 1938), pp. 242-69; Oscar Lange (with Fred M. Taylor and Benjamin E. Lippincott), *On the Economic Theory of Socialism* (St. Paul, 1938); Abba P. Lerner, 'Statics and Dynamics in Socialist Economics,' in *Economic Journal* (1937), p. 253; James Meade and Charles Hitch, *Introduction to Economic Analysis and Policy* (New York, 1938), especially Parts II and III.

vided there are free markets for goods and jobs. But freedom of choice of goods and, to a large extent, of jobs is curtailed in Russia, the former by the price and tax system, the latter by methods of labor recruiting and by the rigidity of planned output.

The only justification for the Russian system of fixed prices and huge sales taxes might lie in the simplicity of this form of revenue collection during hurried industrialization under threat of war. Even this advantage of sales taxes is dubious, although it may have carried some weight in the turmoil of Russian industrial and military expansion begun under conditions of analphabetism and ruin.

Three main complaints can be and have been raised against capitalism: monopoly, unemployment, privileges.

By failing to sell at cost and by adding sales taxes to fixed prices, the Soviet system has maintained one characteristic feature of monopoly: it does not allocate the nation's resources in the way most desirable to the individual consumer-worker. The resources thus imperfectly allocated may nevertheless be fully used: neither men nor machines are idle, although too many are employed–wasted, in a sense–in certain industries, and too few in others, compared with the scale of consumer-worker desires.

Unemployment has to do not with the divorce between current prices and costs caused by price fixation by private or state monopoly, but with future plans, with fears and hopes of employers, be they monopolistic or not. On the face of it, exaggerated and contagious fears and hopes will be smoothed out, chances for continuous planning ahead and therefore for stable employment enhanced, if those who plan are informed of each other's expectations and mutually correct them: a point in favor of centralized planning, of a Gosplan-like clearing house for hopes and fears.

It can be argued, however, that to correct ill-informed, exaggerated expectations, it is not at all necessary to concentrate decisions in one place and take all planning initiative away from individual plant managers. The latter certainly know more about specific opportunities and trends in their fields and are quicker to use them. It is only with regard to the general spending and saving of the people and to the general aims (such as welfare or war) of the people's state, that the top economic officials are probably better informed. To counteract hopes and fears epidemically swaying the whole country, it may suffice to entrust economic officials (as is now done, in fact, in most countries) with the fiscal and monetary machinery to curtail or expand the overall funds available to producers and consumers—and to leave to individuals the decision how best to use the available funds.

In Russia, centralized planning and management happened to be applied not to a slowly growing economy and its fluctuations, but to a rapid State-financed industrial and military expansion, comparable in speed to the present war effort of the United States. In both countries, jobs have been found for all. The disappearance of unemployment in Russia under the Plans is, therefore, no conclusive validation of centralized planning. Unemployment might also have disappeared had funds of the same size come into the hands of freely deciding producers, whether through State orders for investment goods or war goods, or (in the case of another welfare and war policy) through public demand for consumables.

At the same time, the Russian experience gives evidence—partly recorded in this book—of frictions and human deficiencies in the huge machinery so overloaded with responsibilities.

Private monopolies have, however, another feature: monopolistic profits are appropriated by private persons; thus inequalities of income, status, and power are aggravated. This is not perceptible in Russia. Profits do not become private incomes. If there are privileges, they are not because of profits. Nor is it clear whether there are in Russia any other factors which may perpetuate group privileges.

To be sure, rare talents are paid high salaries in Russia—in money or in kind—and extra effort is rewarded by bonus. To ensure a high level of production, hardly any other method could have been devised, except substituting for acquisitive motives those of love of work and self-expression, of ambition and honor and social recognition, or even of a self-effacing sense of duty, patriotism, and idealism. In the United States we know of such substitution. It has been practiced on a large scale in Soviet Russia. Furthermore, opportunities for lucrative private investment are absent. What income inequality remains cannot fully manifest itself in unequal standards of living: luxurious ostentation is not approved by prevailing mores, and, what is more, luxuries, so far, have often been virtually unavailable. All these factors have, no doubt, helped dam inequalities in living conditions while getting the most out of peak abilities and skills. Even so, inequalities are considerable.

But even with equalized consumption levels, there would in any society with divided functions be differences in standing and power. Certain functions imply more leadership than others. The question is whether the differences are growing—they would diminish if educational opportunities were equal—and whether the functional groups can perpetuate themselves, either by inheritance or co-optation.

In the traditional ideology of the ruling Party (whether realized in practice or not), political hegemony belongs—or did so until recently—to industrial manual workers. On the other hand, the official concept of 'Soviet intelligentsia' links together persons with administrative functions, general as well as economic, with those exercising other non-manual skills. Because of the economic and social peculiarities of the system, the following list of 'Soviet intelligentsia' supplied by Premier V. Molotov is of great interest (in particular, some of the sub-items under 1 refer to 'executives' in the American sense, the special subject matter of this book):

Composition of Soviet Intelligentsia on 1 January 1937[2]
(In thousands of persons)

1. Heads of enterprises, institutions, workshops, State farms, collective farms, etc.	1,751
(Heads of administrative, health, and cultural institutions 450	
Directors and heads of State enterprises, workshops, and plant sections, and their deputies 350	
Chairmen and deputy chairmen of collective farms and administrators of auxiliary farms for marketed products 582	
Directors of Machine-Tractor Stations and of State farms, and administrators of auxiliary farms 19	
Heads of industrial co-operatives 40	
Directors and administrators of stores 250	
Directors and administrators of public eating places ...... 60)	
2. Engineers and architects (excluding heads of enterprises and workshops)	250
3. Intermediate technical personnel (engineering aids, foresters, station masters, etc.)	810
4. Agronomists	80
5. Other agricultural specialists (surveyors, animal husbandmen, etc.)	96
6. Science workers (professors and other college instructors, etc.)	80
7. Teachers	969
8. Cultural workers (journalists, librarians, club administrators, etc.)	297
9. Arts workers	159
10. Physicians	132
11. Intermediate medical personnel (medical attendants, midwives, nurses)	382
12. Economists, statisticians	822
13. Bookkeepers, accountants	1,617
14. Justice workers (judges, public prosecutors, etc.)	46
15. College students	550
16. Other groups of intelligentsia (including military[3])	1,550
Grand Total	9,591

Thus out of nearly ten million salary-earners, low and high, constituting the 'Soviet intelligentsia' in 1937, about one and three quarters millions were leading personnel of institutions and enterprises in city and country; of these about a third of a million were industrial managers or their assistants. The author of

[2] V. Molotov, *The Third Five Year Plan*, Address to the 18th Party Congress (Moscow, 1939), pp. 44-5.
[3] Presumably officers.

Chapter IX offers a hypothesis which may perhaps be best formulated as follows: By the time of the outbreak of war, industrial managers had become the nucleus of what might develop into a privileged and ruling class; inequality of educational opportunities tended to make hereditary the power and standing of this group and others that enjoy a similar educational level, exercise functions of leadership, and are related to the managers and to each other by links of family and social intercourse; there are traces of a deliberate policy fostering the formation, consolidation, and rule of this stratum.

The other authors and the present writer have not found this hypothesis sufficiently supported by facts. It has been pointed out that any possible self-perpetuation of a leading stratum must have been of very short duration, not earlier than the last 'purge.' There is some question that educational inequalities existing in Soviet Russia could have this effect of self-perpetuating the leading groups. The system of State scholarships for colleges did equalize training opportunities as much as was possible under conditions of unequal incomes and home backgrounds, short of introducing full State maintenance for all children. In particular, it is questioned whether the failure to provide equal education on a still larger scale, and especially whether the recent raising of college admission requirements (which fell heaviest on young people with poorer home backgrounds), are to be explained by motives other than limitations of State finances and the necessities of war preparation.

The general impression is still that of trial and error. The power of the industrial manager has been repeatedly reduced and again enlarged. Superimposed on the great policy zigzags—War Communism (1918-21) to New Economic Policy (1921-8) to Five Year Plans (1928-)—were numerous minor waves, not always synchronized in all fields. These were partly genuine experiments, successive attempts to find an optimum solution. As often as not, however, the ups and downs reflected political struggles and changes in the balance of power. Distrust of the manager by the Party man periodically flared up and subsided. The general trend, too, which may be discovered behind these fluctuations in managerial status and functions, was economic only in so far as it reflected the natural recovery and consolidation of industry after the First World War and the Revolution, and the gradual training and selection of skills. The sociological and political components of the trend were at least as decisive. The Party which has ruled for a quarter of a century has undergone profound changes both in composition and attitude, while a new generation has grown into positions of industrial leadership.

Full analysis of these fluctuations and trends would have to go far beyond our subject: parallel changes that occurred in general administration, army, education, possibly in arts and mores, would have to be studied to throw more light on this important piece of social history. One of the authors of the present book (Mr. Yugow) deliberately refrained from daring attempts to fathom sociological causes. In the chapters assigned to him, he preferred to describe facts mainly in terms of economic growth, consolidation, experimentation. Another author (Mr. Schwarz) has made such an attempt. His hypotheses and tentative results will be found interesting and provocative, although no ultimate validity can be claimed until further studies and events have provided more solid ground.

This book is not a series of monologues. Its specific approach, the study of managers rather than of the aggregate economy, was suggested by the late Arthur Feiler. He co-ordinated the work in its earlier stages. Feiler was an unbiased and scholarly observer of the Bolshevik experiment.[4] As he was also well-versed in the institutions and techniques of modern capitalism, he could judge Bolshevism on its merits and not by its name. He was as attached

[4] Arthur Feiler, *The Experiment of Bolshevism* (New York, 1930); 'The Soviet Union and the Business Cycle,' in *Social Research* (August 1936), pp. 282-303.

to the cause of freedom and as familiar with the great advantages of free markets and private enterprise as he was anxious to understand the great Revolution. He saw in the problem of industrial and farm managers a clue to understanding both the economics and sociology of modern Russia.

The study of collective farm management [5] was assigned to Mr. Yugow. In the field of industrial management Mr. Bienstock undertook to analyze managerial powers and incentives. Mr. Yugow studied the economics and accountancy of Soviet plants, and Mr. Schwarz the sociological background. These aspects proved to be closely interrelated—hence changes in the original scheme and dual authorship of certain chapters. The final responsibility for each chapter lies, however, with the author or authors indicated by initials in the Table of Contents. The method of procedure has inevitably produced a certain amount of repetition, but it is hoped that this will serve to facilitate an understanding of the problems.

Until 1922 the three authors were outstandingly active in Russian public affairs, as economic and political writers and, temporarily, as officials. Since that time they have lived abroad, but their work has involved daily and thorough study of Russia. Their original insight into their native country and their uninterrupted occupation with it probably make up for the handicap under which they appear to suffer, as compared with some more recent foreign visitors to Russia. Certainly, the reader will do well to consult such outstanding eyewitnesses of Soviet factory life as John Scott.[6] The contribution of our authors is complementary to such reports: it is a systematic analysis of published sources by men who can read between the lines. The reader will be able to gauge the force, maturity, and tranquillity of their

[5] No attempt was made to include a study of the other agricultural production form, the State farm. It was thought that such a study would reveal few problems not shown in an analysis of State industrial plants. For similar reasons, specific study of trade and bank management was also omitted, except where connected with supply and credit problems of industry.

[6] John Scott, *Behind the Urals* (New York, 1942).

judgment and their success in detaching themselves from preconceived views and political bias.

Sources were, in the main, legislative material, including public discussions of Communist Party bodies; extensive economic and legal literature (books, periodicals, and the daily press) on management practice, both general and by industries. This includes illuminating 'self-criticism,' originating in the jealousies or discontent of rivals, subordinates, or customers; it has rightly been called the Soviet surrogate for parliamentary clash of opinions, and must naturally be treated with appropriate circumspection. Finally, use has been made of Soviet fiction. Russian fiction has preserved its naturalistic tradition. Soviet novelists and short-story writers often claim to record social facts quasi-photographically. With all necessary caution, and discounting for official cant, we may learn from them much about the people, or at least about what models the State holds up to them.

All these sources require delicate and cautious treatment. Even in legal and statistical matters, the great gaps and contradictions, and the fluidity of concepts characteristic of Russian sources are perplexing to the Westerner. For example, it has proved impossible for Mr. Yugow to compile a complete statistical picture of actual revenues and costs, and of the sources and allocation of profits, subsidies, capital reserves, and turnover tax, of Soviet industry for a single year or a five-year period, not to speak of a series of years. There is nothing comparable either to published reports of American corporations or to detailed estimated breakdowns of national income and expenditure. To be sure, Soviet censorship has occasionally been relaxed in order to provide publicity material to some outstanding official: this gives the student important information which may be fitted into the picture with ingenuity and circumspection.

The three authors of the study and the writer of the present introduction have continually interchanged hypotheses and evidence, criticisms and suggestions. Common ground was often found when misunderstandings were weeded out. In a few cases, however, where the problem is too delicate or complicated to be finally tested with the material in hand, an author presents his working hypothesis, clearly designating it as such, and accepting sole responsibility for it. Even so, discussion of the hypothesis always helped locate the essential remaining unknowns.

PART I

MANAGEMENT IN INDUSTRY

I

Organs of Industrial Management

a. Development and Structure

As State-owned industry was consolidated and expanded under Soviet rule, principles and forms of industrial management underwent many changes and fluctuations, only the most important of which will be treated in this book.[1] In the present chapter, we shall study the changing relations—and conflicts—between the various State organs of industrial management in and outside plants. Indecision—and some struggle—prevailed concerning principles of organization (was it to be by industries or by geographical areas?), and concerning the question of strict industrial centralization as opposed to some plant autonomy.

In the first years after the nationalization of industry, management was controlled by a territorial 'Economic Council' in each large city and in almost each of the seventy-eight provinces (the Czarist *guberniya*, abolished in 1936). The Economic Councils were attached to the corresponding organs of local or regional administration, the *Soviets* (Councils) of Workers and Peasants. In addition, all large and medium-sized plants were organized by industries and controlled by Main Industrial Boards (committees) or *Glavks*. Both Glavks and territorial Economic Councils were, in theory, subordinate to the Supreme Economic Council of the U.S.S.R. Throughout the years of the Civil War and economic collapse, however, organization by industries was rather nominal. The inter-regional economic nexus and local contacts with the

[1] 'Industry' is used in this study in its narrower sense, and thus does not include agriculture, trade, or transportation.

central government were very weak. Accordingly, local Soviets and their organs, the local Economic Councils, had greater opportunities than did the Main Boards of individual industries, impotent in remote Moscow offices and unable to provide fuel, raw materials, food, or transportation.

Gradually, however, as the central power became stronger around 1922, and as the economic structure gained in cohesion under the New Economic Policy (the NEP, 1921-8) the territorial Economic Councils were pushed aside, while national consolidation of individual industries progressed. In 1923 the functions of provincial and municipal Economic Councils were ordered restricted to small industries of local significance. The administration of medium-sized and large industry was ordered more effectively centralized in the Supreme Economic Council, its industrial divisions (Glavks), and the territorial or industrial subdivisions of the latter, the 'Trusts.' But this centralized machine did not work adequately and had to be reorganized again and again.

New Glavks were created, small ones merged into larger ones. Plants were transferred from one Glavk to another. In 1932 the Supreme Economic Council was split into three large industrial *Narkomats* or People's Commissariats, one for Heavy Industry, one for Light Industry, and one for the Lumber Industry. The food industry had earlier (1930) been placed in a special People's Commissariat for Supply, which also controlled the storage and distribution of farm products. Step by step, more People's Commissariats were created by splitting up old ones, until, in 1943, there were twenty-five industrial People's Commissariats. The governments of the constituent Republics have People's Commissariats of their own for certain industries.

Since 1940, the administration of industry has, on the whole, been organized as follows:

SUPREME ORGANS OF INDUSTRIAL ADMINISTRATION IN THE U.S.S.R.

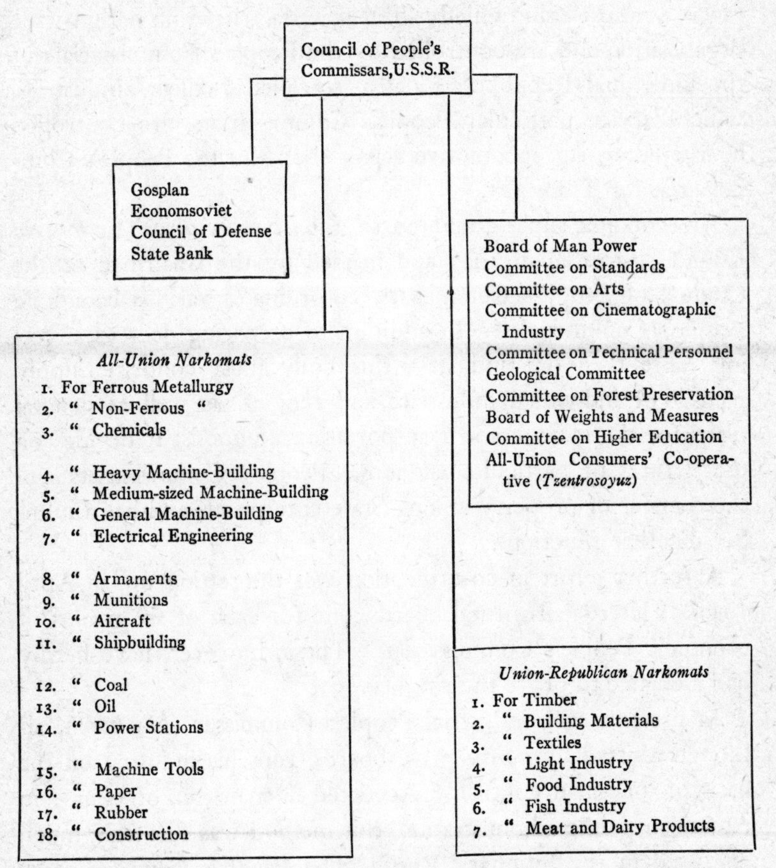

In some constituent Republics there exist, in addition, People's Commissariats for 'local industry' and 'local fuel industry,' which have no corresponding organs in the Union administration.

The more important industries are directly controlled by the so-called 'All-Union People's Commissariats,' without intermediate organs of the constituent Republics. Other industries are controlled by Union Commissariats known as 'Union-Republican People's Commissariats,' which control not directly but through analogous People's Commissariats of the constituent Republics.

Such is, in particular, the case in mass consumption industries (food, textiles). Small industries and handicrafts of local importance, or those using chiefly local materials, have no nation-wide organization and are controlled by the People's Commissariats of the individual Republics. Finally, so-called auxiliary industries, which service particular People's Commissariats, are controlled by the latter, e.g. locomotive repair shops by the People's Commissariat for Transport.

An economic super-commissariat, the *Economsoviet* (Economic Council), created in 1937 and headed by the Chairman of the Council of People's Commissars, co-ordinates various economic People's Commissariats.[2] In addition to preparing decrees affecting more than one industry, this body must confirm 'supply plans' [3] of individual industries and regions, as well as general plans for the storage and transportation of goods. It decides on the statutes of particular economic People's Commissariats and the transfer of property among State enterprises, and has a number of other functions.

A further effort in co-ordination was the setting up, in April 1940, of interdepartmental boards, one for each of six groups of economic People's Commissariats.[4] These, however, have hardly had a chance to prove their utility.

At present, each industrial People's Commissar (*Narkom*), although assisted by consultative boards, runs his industry on the basis of 'one-man control.' [5] Accepted as a matter of course in American public administration, this method was formerly much discussed in revolutionary Russia. The People's Commissar ap-

[2] Decree of 23 November 1937. The Council of Labor and Defense created during the Civil War (30 November 1918) had, on the whole, the same functions as the Economsoviet of 1937.

[3] Cf. Chapter v.

[4] Decree of 15 April 1940. The groups were as follows: metallurgy and chemistry, machine-building, defense industry, fuel and power, mass consumption foods, agriculture and *zagotovki* (collection and storage of farm products).

[5] *Yedino-natchaliye*, literally, single supervision, rule or authority. See 'Control' under Note on Terminology and Citations, above.

points and issues orders to the heads of Glavks and Trusts and to managers of larger plants. He has power to dismiss them. This is mentioned here to emphasize at the outset the fact that the typical manager of a Russian industrial plant is a State official. This well-known fact will be seen to involve a number of problems.

Each industrial People's Commissariat is divided into Glavks for sub-industries, or for areas, or both. Large Glavks are, in turn, subdivided into Trusts. The managers of most industrial plants are directly subordinate to and appointed by the Glavks or Trusts.

A typical People's Commissariat (or Glavk, or Trust) would have these departments: technical, planning, finance, supply and sale, construction, manpower, accounting. In the first period of centralized industrial management (1920-33) each of these so-called 'functional' departments controlled directly the activities of the corresponding department of subordinate plants. This practice, chaotic and cumbersome, was stopped by a decision of the Communist Party Congress (1934), which strengthened the one-man control of both the plant manager and the chief of the People's Commissariat (or Glavk, or Trust).[6]

Of the two administrative links intermediate between the People's Commissariat and a typical plant—the Glavk and the Trust—one (generally the Trust) was recently (1936-40) suppressed in certain industries. This long-overdue simplification responded, in part at least, to certain changes in the structure of production. Parallel with the development of highly specialized plants was an increase in co-operation between plants producing similar goods (the aim being to secure better utilization of equipment) and between plants supplying and those receiving raw materials or semi-finished goods. There grew in importance a new, complex type of plant, the *Kombinat*, which produces a wide range of goods based on a single main raw material, with its by-products and waste. The largest Soviet plants are such combines, among them

[6] 17th Party Congress, p. 673. See also c, below, on the 'functional' system in plants.

Dnepro Kombinat (based on water power), Magnitogorski Kombinat (based on iron ore), and Bereznikovski Kombinat (based on potassium). Obviously, neither plants heavily involved in mutual co-operation nor, *a fortiori*, 'combines' with diversified production can be successfully controlled by such highly specialized agencies as the Trusts.

b. Plant Management vs. Higher Organs of State Industry

The basic production unit, the 'plant' or 'enterprise,' is never easily defined. Precision is particularly difficult in the case of the U.S.S.R., where the nationalization of all important economic activities has done away with many old legal concepts without creating exact substitutes. In the terminology of Russian official statistics, an independent industrial plant (*predpriyatiye*, literally enterprise) has its own balance sheet and plan of production and finance; some fixed capital (machines, building) and working capital; and an independent current account at the State Bank.[7]

The 'director' or manager is the leading official of a plant and the recognized representative of its interests, especially in matters concerning its property.

Relations between plant management and higher agencies of economic administration, the limits of the autonomy of a plant manager, present one of the most complicated and acute problems of all Soviet economy. Although plant management has been repeatedly declared 'autonomous' to a considerable degree, it is not only an element in a tremendous State economic hierarchy but it is also subject to a changing degree of Party control, if no longer of labor-union control.[8]

In matters affecting plant property, the manager's powers are very limited, indeed. His formal right to 'administer' (*rasporyazhat'sya*) the State-owned property of the plant is, as a rule, rec-

[7] A. D. Mikhailov, *Industrial Statistics* (Moscow, 1939), pp. 12-13. On the plant's own 'production and finance plan' see Chapter IV.d. See also 'Plant' in Note on Terminology and Citations, above.

[8] Cf. Chapters II and III.

ognized in official regulations. This right, however, is much narrower than the word might suggest, and does not include the right to sell products except on the basis of a sales contract approved or even drawn by the proper Glavk or People's Commissariat. He may acquire property for the plant only within a supply budget approved by the Glavk or People's Commissariat,[9] except that, in extraordinary cases, he may acquire necessary equipment costing not more than 200 roubles. Nor is he entitled to sell or barter equipment or materials without the special permission of the Economsoviet. Numerous violations or evasions of this last rule were noted by the Communist Party Conference of 1941, which found that 'many plants and railroads often sell allegedly superfluous equipment as materials.' A severe decree issued in consequence declared sale by plant directors of machines, equipment, raw material, and fuel to be 'plunder of socialist property,' i.e. a crime.[10]

True, high organs of State and Party have more than once declared that the plant manager should have full autonomy in the field of production, within the limits of the national Plan and of government decrees. As early as 1934, the government approved 'Model Statutes for Plants in Heavy Industry,' drafted by a conference of managers of large plants and giving them considerable autonomy.[11] But, in practice, the personnel of the Glavks and People's Commissariats persistently interfere with current work of plants. The limits of plant autonomy have never been generally determined with any definiteness. The Soviet economic press repeatedly gives space to public discussions of this question.

In the fall of 1940, managers of four important Leningrad plants published in *Pravda* an 'open letter' which probably voiced the sentiment of many Soviet managers.[12] The writers find that Party and State expect managers to manage plants 'with authority

[9] For details, cf. Chapter v.

[10] Decree of the Presidium of the Supreme Soviet of the U.S.S.R., 10 February 1941.

[11] Published in *Steel* (1934), No. 11-12, pp. 106-11.

[12] 'On the One-Man Control of the Manager,' *Pravda,* 10 September 1940.

and sovereignty.' However, 'the established practice of interrelations between managers of our plants and the Glavks and People's Commissariats is often inconsistent with these demands of Party and State.' The letter points out the chief limitations on the manager's authority. He is, in the first place, restrained in the distribution of the 'fund for wages and salaries' (i.e. the pay-roll budget, fixed in advance for a certain period) among the various categories of employees. Nor is he free in the allotment of 'the manager's fund' (i.e. the sum provided for employees' bonuses).[13] The Glavks or People's Commissariats, complains the letter, go beyond their duty of fixing in advance the plant's manpower and pay roll, and take it on themselves to allocate pay roll among main categories (manual workers, engineers and technicians, office workers, and maintenance workers). The manager is thus deprived of the flexibility necessary to use to the best possible purpose the total amount available. If, while fulfilling his production assignment, the manager finds it possible to reduce working personnel during a quarter in order to accumulate a reserve for efficiency bonuses, the Glavk or People's Commissariat responds by cutting the total allowance for wages and salaries for the remainder of the year. The Glavks also allocate bonuses among categories of employees in advance, thus often preventing managers from encouraging their most talented and useful employees properly and promptly. Greater freedom in using the 'fund for wages' and the 'manager's fund' is demanded.

Also harmful are restraints placed on purchases, especially the clause requiring special permission for purchases exceeding 200 roubles. Greater flexibility is sought: the open letter proposes that managers be given the right to buy urgently needed equipment with profits that have accrued from over-fulfilment of Plan and which remain at the disposal of the plant management.[14]

[13] The wages and salaries 'fund' is determined by the plant's 'technical-financial plan' (see Chapter IV). Overdrawing within any quarter is a punishable offense.

[14] For a more detailed discussion of profits, see Chapter VI.

The letter of the four managers was sympathetically received by both *Pravda* and industrial periodicals. Prominent representatives of the Party and government took up the objections to the 'narrow-minded tutelage' of Glavks over plants. Five months later (February 1941), the 18th Party Conference still found cause to declare that the 'People's Commissariats and Glavks are in many respects working bureaucratically' and that 'the manager should be enabled to run the plant with full powers, and should be entirely responsible for its condition and work.' [15]

Not only the manager's power but his very position has been highly unstable. Frequent reshuffling and removal of managers make plant autonomy difficult to achieve. Not many managers have the will to struggle for 'autonomy' when, as Stalin put it in March 1939, 'dozens and hundreds of managers and engineers . . . were transferred senselessly from one position to another and back.' [16] For example, in the Voroshilovugol' Kombinat (coal mining), 'almost one-third of the pit directors and chief pit engineers were removed in the first half of 1940 . . . The leading managers often have no time to gather experience . . . The ridiculous merry-go-round of thoughtless, wanton shuffling, dismissals and appointments continues.' [17]

Thus, the highest organs of State and Party have for several years proclaimed that plant management should be relieved of narrow-minded tutelage and be given necessary autonomy. At the same time, leading officials of the same government, leading Communists, People's Commissars, and Glavk chiefs infringed on autonomy and hobbled plant management in all its activities. This stubborn contradiction had many roots. In the first place, owing to persistent struggles among official organs, the legal norms regulating interrelations between higher and lower State agencies were, quite generally, accepted in practice only slowly. This was especially true of relations between individual links of the eco-

[15] 18th Party Conference, pp. 5 and 11.
[16] 18th Party Congress, p. 29.
[17] *Pravda*, 1 July 1940.

nomic hierarchy: neither law nor contract could effectively settle their respective rights and duties under conditions of rapid industrialization and general administrative turmoil. Plants could not become autonomous in fact so long as many were unable to carry out their plans and needed the help of higher organs to overcome repeated hitches in production. Last but not least, many managers lacked the ability and background necessary to run an autonomous plant.

Only in recent years, as Soviet industry has become stronger and its leading personnel has improved by selection and training, have some plant managers won autonomy and made effective the theoretical rights and powers decreed earlier by Party and government.[18] They won, particularly, greater freedom to purchase raw materials and equipment.[19] Under the pressure of well-managed plants, the number of links in the economic hierarchy was in many places reduced, and plants were relieved of much of the old 'narrow-minded tutelage.'

c. Plant Manager and Assistants

If the 'autonomy' of the plant manager in relation to higher agencies of industrial management is still far from real, how does he get on with the leading plant personnel, i.e. in how far is he the 'boss'?

The 'Model Statutes for Plants in Heavy Industry,' approved as early as 1934, describe the manager as 'chief leader of the plant and main organizer of production . . . ; his orders are to be fulfilled without fail by all personnel of the plant as well as by all persons working on the premises of the plant.' [20]

Since that time, all relevant decisions of Congresses and Conferences of the Communist Party have been based on recognition of the manager's full and exclusive power within the plant. 'Each plant has a leader endowed with full power of decision, hence

[18] Cf. Chapter IX.

[19] Cf. Chapter V.

[20] *Steel* (1934), No. 11-12, p. 110.

fully responsible for everything: the plant manager,' declares an official manual.[21]

Apart from subordination to higher industrial agencies, and the influence of Party organs, the manager has, in fact, full independence in dealing with his subordinates. His orders are compulsory for all employees of the plant. He sets tasks for all its divisions and supervises their fulfilment. He selects the leading engineer and technical staff as well as bookkeepers, economists, etc., although appointments of the higher personnel must be approved by the Glavk or People's Commissariat.

Even this authority of the manager has been the result of a slow process of development. During the 1920's, when few technically qualified managers were trusted by the Soviet government, the manager was under detailed and, in general, 'narrow-minded' supervision on the part of local Party 'cells' and labor unions with whom he was supposed to carry out 'triangular' co-operation.[22] In addition, at about the same period, the manager was really dependent on his technical assistants. In the first years after the nationalization of industry, the plant manager was usually a Communist, the so-called 'Red Manager,' and his lack of training put technical management into the hands of the engineers. Less frequently, a non-Party expert would be appointed manager with a Communist alternate or assistant acting as a vigilant 'commissar,' analogous to the political commissars of the Red Army. In neither case was there, of course, 'one-man control.' The peculiar dualism between the manager and his staff added to the chaos and irresponsibility of the triangle formed by the manager, the representatives of the Party, and the unions. This state of affairs no longer exists. The technical staff is now fully subordinated to the manager. As a result of the general rise of technical education and environment, the manager has, as a rule, the necessary technical training. Typically, the present-day manager is a relatively

[21] Economic Institute of the Academy of Sciences, *Economics of Socialist Industry* (Moscow, 1940), p. 579.

[22] Cf. Chapters II and III.

young man, brought up under the Soviet regime. He is almost always a member of the Communist Party.[23] The 'triangle,' too, has practically disappeared.

As mentioned above,[24] most plants as well as higher industrial agencies were for a long time managed on the 'functional' system, i.e. various managerial functions were divided among various plant 'departments.' For instance, in a metallurgical plant, a plant planning and production department would lay out the production program for the foundry section. Planned production costs of the foundry would be determined by the plant's 'department of economy.' The amount of needed materials would be fixed by the supply departments. The scale of wages and the norms of labor efficiency would be fixed by the department of wage rates. Still another department would hire and fire foundry workers. The chief of the foundry section, under these circumstances, had little power or responsibility; he merely co-ordinated the orders of other departments.

At that time the plant manager could manage the plant only nominally; real management was in the hands of the functional departments headed by assistant managers. In some plants there were fourteen or fifteen such quasi-independent assistant managers 'co-ordinated' by the manager. The management of several big coal pits in the Donbas was divided among twenty-two heads of functional departments: each worked in the head office and had a representative in the pit.[25]

In 1934, the 'functional system,' was suppressed: the 17th Congress resolved 'to do away with the functional system in . . . all Soviet economic organs and to reshape them . . . on the basis of production-territorial principles, beginning with the lowest production links and up to the People's Commissariat,' [26] i.e. to divide

[23] Cf. Chapter II.
[24] Chapter I.a.
[25] L. M. Kaganovich, 'On the Working of the Donbas Coal Industry,' *Pravda*, 9 April 1933.
[26] 17th Party Congress, p. 672.

power according to location or type of product, and not according to function.

It was obviously impossible to install the new production-territorial system in pure form. Acquisition of materials, hiring, bookkeeping, have to remain in the hands of functional divisions of a plant. But the head of the section or workshop, the foreman, the 'shock brigader' have acquired larger responsibilities. Functional departments diminished in size and began to operate through the heads of sections, foremen, etc.

Most important, the manager became the only person responsible for the operation of the plant in all its subdivisions. The manager's authority within the plant has increased. He rules the whole production process, bears responsibility for the technological process, for quantitative fulfilment of the plan, and for the quality of goods produced—though in large plants, responsibilities in the production field are, in actual fact, shared with the chief engineer. In a typical large plant the following departments would be directly subordinated to the manager's office: accounting, planning, finance, procurement, sales.[27] The chief accountant, formerly the eye of the higher administration, is now subordinated to the manager, although some peculiarities of his position persist.[28] The chief engineer typically has under his supervision the chief technologist, the head of the design bureau, the head of the power plant, the chief construction engineer, the chief of technical supervision, and the chiefs of sections or workshops.

One of the manager's deputies usually heads a 'labor and wages department'; but the manager himself is responsible for promotion and assignments of technical personnel and employees in general. He determines, within a fairly wide framework of rules,[29] the scale of wages and the norms of piece work, organizes train-

[27] N. A. Blatov, *Principles of Industrial Accounting and Calculation* (Moscow, 1939), pp. 18-19.
[28] Cf. Chapter VI.b.2.
[29] Cf. Chapter III.

ing, directs 'socialist competition,' and is responsible for measures protecting labor's health and welfare.

The leaders of Soviet economy have admitted more than once —even after the reform of 1934—that plant management was unwieldy and bureaucratic. The question of reorganization was raised anew in 1938 and described then as acute and inescapable. Before the war with Germany, suggestions were made to increase further the independence of the plant in its current work (i.e. within the framework of the general Plan) and to strengthen the internal powers of managers. With the outbreak of war, public discussion of the problem was postponed; of course, further reorganization may have been achieved without such discussion.

II

Industrial Management and the Communist Party

a. The Communist Party in Economic Control

AT the beginning of 1939, the Communist Party had close to 2,500,000 members and candidates for membership, almost all either manual or white-collar workers. Since there were 28,000,000 manual and white-collar workers in the country,[1] Party members constituted approximately 8 per cent of this group. This minority occupies the most important positions.

Active Party control of every manifestation of public life is inherent in the Soviet system. Article 126 of the 1936 Constitution of the U.S.S.R. calls the Communist Party the 'vanguard of the working people in their struggle to strengthen and develop the socialist system.' The Party 'is the leading core of all organizations of the working people, both public and State.' [2] According to its statutes, 'the Party leads the working class, the farmers, the intelligentsia, in short, the whole Soviet people . . .' [3]

In 1934, at the 17th Party Congress, L. M. Kaganovich, a member of the highest Party organ, the *Politburo* (Political Bureau) of the Central Committee, described one of its tasks as 'operative' (current) management of socialist construction.[4] Through individual Party members, tiny wheels in a gigantic machine, the

[1] 18th Party Congress, pp. 24, 147.
[2] *Constitution of the U.S.S.R.* (New York, 1943).
[3] 18th Party Congress, pp. 6ff.
[4] 17th Party Congress, pp. 563-4.

Party controls industry day by day. The Politburo regularly discusses reports on single industries or large plants.

A specifically Soviet expression is *proverka ispolneniya* (check-up of tasks performed), carried out by the Party. At the 17th Congress, Stalin asked for 'systematic' supervision as against 'chance' check-ups of industry; such supervision would 'prevent the violation of decisions of the Party and the Soviet government.' 'A well-organized check-up of tasks performed is a searchlight which helps throw light upon the work of the [managerial] apparatus at all times and exposes Jacks-in-office and red-tape.' [5]

The forms in which the Party's economic control is exercised have varied through the years. The 17th Party Congress (1934) decided to attach special industrial divisions to the Central Committee of the Party of the U.S.S.R., as well as to regional Party committees. These were to be subdivided by industries.[6] All Party organizations were directed to supervise energetically and systematically the activities of economic organs.

At the beginning of 1937, however, Stalin admonished Party organizations not to play themselves up as 'substitutes for economic organs'; the latter must not be 'depersonalized.' Party organizations 'must guide economic activities, not leaving economic organs out of the picture but through these very organs.' [7]

The 18th Congress (1939) again discussed relations between the Party and economic organs. 'The industrial divisions of the Party do not know what they really have to do,' said Zhdanov, one of the most important members of the Politburo, at one time regarded as Stalin's heir presumptive. 'They are allowing themselves to become substitutes for economic management and to compete with it. All this leads to depersonalization and irresponsibility.' Accordingly, the Congress decided to abolish the industrial divi-

[5] 17th Party Congress, pp. 34-5.

[6] Art. 25 of the Party Statutes of 1934: 17th Party Congress, p. 676.

[7] J. Stalin, *Address to the Plenary Meeting of the Central Committee of the Communist Party, February-March* 1937 (Moscow, 1937), p. 5.

sions attached to Party committees. Interpreting the decisions of this Congress, an official manual says:

> One-man control implies strict demarcation between the administration, on the one hand, and Party and trade-union organizations on the other. This strict demarcation must be applied on all levels of industrial management. Current operations in fulfilment of Plan are the task of the administration. The chief of a workshop, the manager of the plant, the head of the Glavk, have full powers, each within his field, and the Party and trade-union organizations may not interfere with their orders.[8]

Yet, at Zhdanov's suggestion, the same 18th Congress granted the 'primary Party organizations,' i.e. Party organizations in plants, the right to supervise management, and introduced the ruling formally into the Party statutes.[9] Zhdanov was fully aware of a conflict between one-man control and the form of supervision he suggested. 'During the discussion, voices claimed that to grant the right of supervision to primary Party organizations is to strike a blow at one-man control.'

> [But] those people who think that one-man control consists in dominating the factory without having the help of the active workers do not understand the essence of one-man control . . . Our Soviet, Bolshevik one-man control consists in being able to give effective orders, organize, select workers, . . . do away with irresponsibility and depersonalization. But, at the same time, management must be able to base this work on the Party organization, the active members of the plant and its whole collective.

Zhdanov praised the Party organization for reorganizing the entire management of the huge Yaroslavl Rubber Combine.

> The Party organization was able to place Party personnel in such a position that it could know exactly what was happening in any

[8] Economic Institute of the Academy of Sciences, *Economics of Socialist Industry* (Moscow, 1940), p. 563.

[9] Art. 61: 'In order to increase the significance of primary Party organizations and their responsibility for the running of productive enterprises . . . the right to supervise the management of such enterprises . . . is granted these organizations.'

department of the plant. The district Party committee and the Party organization [in the plant] did not assume the position of management—on the contrary, [they] provided all the necessary conditions for the free development of independent and creative activity on the part of the managers. But the Party organization was informed of every step of management and, being well informed on plant affairs, directed, instructed and helped management when necessary.[10]

Zhdanov further pointed out that there were hundreds of similar instances of a 'fair combination of Party and economic activity in the life of the primary Party organization.'

At the end of 1939 there was apparently much anxiety in leading Party circles about the shortcomings of industrial management, and an active attitude was asked of Party organizations. Symptomatic of this preoccupation are the November 1939 decisions of the Central Committee, 'On Party work among the masses in the Donbas coal pits' and 'On Party control of ferrous metallurgy enterprises in Donbas and the Chelyabinsk province.'[11] Both are permeated with the idea of daily intervention by the Party (through either primary or local organs). The first resolution plainly puts responsibility for plant effectiveness on the Party organizations within the plant. The Party organizations of the Donbas 'are not executing the decisions of the 18th Party Congress, which charged them with responsibility for the working of plants . . .' The second resolution speaks of the necessity

of securing the daily guidance of every metallurgical plant, of every section, pit, quarry, by provincial, city and district Party committees . . . to make it the obligation of provincial Party committees to inform Party organizations and all individual Communists as to their specific duty in securing normal plant operation in every rolling mill, blast and open-hearth furnace . . . [It is necessary] to secure the active participation of primary Party organizations in the production life of plants and to put into prac-

[10] 18th Party Congress, pp. 534, 535.
[11] 4 and 9 November 1939, published in *Party Construction* (1939), No. 21, pp. 55-8.

tice their right to control plant management, to increase the influence of Party organizations and their responsibility for plant operation.

In fact, the appointment of the plant's managerial personnel is not independent of the Party. If suggestions of the Party organization in the plant are not accepted by the manager, the former may appeal to higher Party organizations, such as the local or provincial Party committee, or the Party organization attached to the Glavk or People's Commissariat. Thus, pressure can be brought to bear on the manager, though formally he remains fully responsible to the regular industrial organs of the State (People's Commissariat, etc.) even if he acts under the pressure of Party regulations.

The 18th Party Conference (February 1941, only two years after the 18th Congress) again stressed the necessity of active intervention of Party organizations in management. After these two years of experimentation, the Politburo, in the person of G. Malenkov, came back to the idea of attaching one or more special industrial secretaries to each regional or local Party committee, at least in highly industrialized areas.[12] The Conference accepted the suggestion and declared regional and local Party committees 'responsible for the working of all industrial and transport enterprises of town and province.' Further,

> it is necessary that Party organizations systematically 'bore into' the affairs of industrial plants . . . and help directors in their daily work of industrial . . . management. It is necessary that Party organizations help the People's Commissariats and Glavks in controlling plant directors . . . The [Party] secretaries for industry must be thoroughly acquainted with what is happening in plants. They must call on them regularly . . . to discover shortcomings in plant operation and to strive to do away with such shortcomings.

[12] Resolution of the 18th Party Conference, *Bolshevik* (1941), No. 3-4, pp. 30ff.

Specifically, local and regional Party committees, while supervising in detail a plant's current work, must abstain from issuing direct orders of their own.[13] Primary (plant) Party organizations may report plant shortcomings to local or regional Party committees. The manager must answer such accusations and carry out the resulting decisions of the committee. Orders concerning the plant are issued in his name alone, however.

Thus the Communist Party has repeatedly changed its official attitude on the relation between Party agencies and industrial management. The basic principle of the Party's economic sovereignty, laid down in 1934, was somewhat vaguely interpreted in 1937 and 1939 so as to prevent outright interference by primary and local Party agencies. Only a few months later, the lag in coal production inspired new Party resolutions, restoring at least in part the power of the lower Party organs. This control was further strengthened in 1941 when new decisions, arising perhaps from the requirements of the approaching war, sought to combine the Party's supervisory powers with the 'full authority' of the plant director. All this appears to be a most delicate and complicated form of collaboration. It is probable that collaboration is now more effective than before, mainly because most managers are now Communists and often members of the local and regional Party committees.[14]

b. Party Guidance in Practice

Principles established and frequently changed by the highest Party organs have been complicated enough. Party guidance in practice, even more inconsistent than in theory, will be illustrated by a few instances from every-day plant life. In judging them, the reader must remember to discount for subjective elements in the sources quoted.

The first secretary of a provincial Party committee (*obkom*) is, for all practical purposes, the real boss of the province. He is

[13] Ibid., pp. 58ff.
[14] See c, below.

also the chief controller and inspector of all its industrial plants. The scope of his and his committee's responsibility is very wide. For instance, the Party Central Committee, in its decision of 25 October 1940, pointed out that the real cause for the unsatisfactory development of the Archangel timber industry was the fact that the Party committee of the province lost contact with the management.[15]

The obkom must, from time to time, intervene directly in the management of this or that important plant. The Secretary of the Yaroslavl obkom, N. Patolichev, relates that, in line with the instructions of the Party Central Committee, the obkom investigated the operation of the big machine-building works at Rybinsk on the Volga: 'The work of the Party organization took on a more concrete character. We now judge the success of Party work by the fulfilment of the plant's daily program . . . The Party organization carried out a big task in curtailing time for the manufacture of certain acutely needed machine parts.'[16]

A. Rozhkov, of the Rostov obkom, regards it as his main task to be in the swim of production at the various plants of his province, to correct shortcomings, and to give concrete assistance to primary Party organizations and managers in directing production.[17]

Some local (city or district) Party committees also seem to play an active role in the management of plants in their territory. The Komsomolski district Party committee earned the praise of the provincial Party committee for its 'concrete work.' Railway cars were standing idle instead of transporting peat to a big electric power station.

It was, of course, possible to have the manager report [to the Party committee], to reprimand him, to make a decision to eliminate immediately the cause of such a situation. Such decisions are frequent in the practice of many town and district Party com-

[15] *Party Construction* (1940), No. 23-4, p. 16.
[16] Ibid. (1941), No. 2, p. 40.
[17] Ibid. (1940), No. 21, p. 53.

mittees. But the Komsomolski district Party committee acted otherwise. In order to find causes, the district committee summoned a conference of dispatchers and engineers on duty. After having checked the situation in full detail, the district committee made a decision in which it pointed out to the power station management measures necessary for doing away with this defect. Very soon the idle cars were moved.[18]

Thus, in practice, the local committee shares managerial responsibility: 'The Kharkov and Dnepropetrovsk city committees of the Communist Party ought to know that, together with the plant managers, they are directly responsible for the operation of plants and factories.' [19]

A few impressions from single factories: To a *Pravda* correspondent, the central figure of the ship-building works in Vladivostok appears to be Y. Ushakov, the secretary of the shipyard's Party organization. The heads of the sections and the engineers call almost daily at his office. 'All these people have, of course, already called at various departments of the management. Yet they consider it their duty to be sure to call at the office of the Party committee.' [20] A non-Party section chief, engineer *A*, was asked by Ushakov to make a report on various shortcomings in the section; thenceforth this engineer was a standing guest of the Party committee. The manager was never mentioned in his report, but the *Pravda* correspondent apparently finds this quite natural and makes no comment on the fact.

At the Kirov (former Putilov) machine-building works in Leningrad, one of the largest industrial plants of the Soviet Union, the plant's Party organization has, according to its acting secretary, direct supervision of the 'carrying out of the industrial program' and 'must solve many questions of everyday work. We have established close contact and unity of action with the man-

[18] Ibid. (1940), No. 23-4, pp. 20-21.

[19] Resolution of the plenary meeting of the Central Committee of the Communist Party of the Ukraine, November 1940; *Party Construction* (1940), No. 23-4, p. 14.

[20] *Pravda*, 7 July 1940, p. 3.

agement. But this does not mean that the Party organization must not influence individual managers by its authority . . .[21]

The Party committee of the big Molotov Automobile Works in Gorki often summoned the designers and 'helped carry out in time the plans of the design bureau.' [22] The Party committee of the Moscow metallurgical and machine-building plant, Sickle and Hammer, received a report from the chief accountant, and at another meeting heard the manager of the local branch of the State Bank.[23]

Thus the primary Party organization in the plant, although officially without executive power, frequently seems to be regarded as a part of industrial management. The old 'Party cell'—of which more presently [24]—had theoretically more power, but since it consisted, as a rule, of technically more or less incompetent people, its interference could, in practice, be only sporadic. The plant Party committee of the late thirties, on the contrary, often consists of experienced and skilled workers and, in part, of engineers. Of 1,300 workers and salaried employees at the Presnya Machine-Building Works (Moscow), 119 were Party members. Of these, more than 100 were engineers, technicians, and other salaried employees, 26 of them working in the plant's management office. Only about 12 Party members were manual workers. The heads of plant sections, their assistants, the foremen, and the inspectors were Communists.[25] In other plants the proportions may be less striking,[26] but the general tendency can hardly be doubted.

[21] A. Sharkov, acting secretary of the Party committee of the Kirov Works, in *Party Construction* (1940), No. 23-4, pp. 31, 33.

[22] M. Radionov, secretary of the provincial Party committee, in *Party Construction* (1941), No. 2, p. 45.

[23] *Party Construction* (1941), No. 2, p. 49.

[24] See c, below.

[25] *Pravda*, 23 July 1940.

[26] The Magnitogorsk rolling-mill '500,' described by John Scott in *Behind the Urals* (New York, 1942; pp. 145-6, 151), had (1935-6) 685 manual and 35 non-manual workers; the Party organization, with 56 members and candidates, and 21 'sympathizers,' included 11 engineers and foremen. That

The examples adduced, the decrees, articles, and reports originating from Party members, indicate that Party agencies have continued to interfere with management. Today, however, most managers are members of the regional or local Party committee, and their one-man control is correspondingly stronger. Moreover, the Party organization at the plant is strictly subordinated to higher (city, district, regional) Party organs. The relation between the manager and Party agencies, the definition of their respective powers and responsibilities, does not give rise to as much tension as it did earlier.

c. The Background

The foregoing review of relations between the Communist Party and industrial management since about 1934 may be better understood against the background of relations between plant managers and secretaries of Party organizations in plants [27] in earlier years.

In theory both the manager and Party secretary in the plant represent economic interests of the State. Nevertheless, there was tension for years. Only around the mid-thirties did it begin visibly to abate. It was not completely eliminated until the forties.

Conflicts between various organs or departments of administration may, of course, be interpreted as bureaucratic rivalry, well known in all countries. In the U.S.S.R. such rivalry existed, e.g. between regional and industrial sub-divisions of State economic organs, or between their lower and upper links.[28] There is, however, sufficient evidence to suggest that the early tension between managers and Party cells was more than an interdepartmental struggle. Its gradual disappearance seems to reflect an important sociological trend. Although the trend was occasionally over-

famous mill, however, was operated by selected personnel, and the high percentage of Communists among its manual workers is likely to represent the extreme opposite to conditions in the Presnya Works.

[27] Called, down to the early thirties, the Party cells.

[28] See Chapter 1.

emphasized in the literature on the subject, antagonism between two social types, the economic official and the Party man, was no legend. At the beginning, the two kinds of jobs could be filled only by two kinds of men, a difference that later disappeared.

During the period of the New Economic Policy (1921-8), the majority of Party officials did not, could not, resemble managers. Generally younger than the managers, most of them had joined the movement in the years of the Revolution, receiving their political education in the school of the Civil War, which deeply affected their thinking and feeling. They regarded themselves more as attackers than as builders. They had a vague feeling that training or practical experience made the managers and the 'old' specialists somehow objectively superior to them, and this stimulated them to emphasize their own 'proletarian' character—real or alleged—especially since it was then a great advantage in the Party to be or to have been a manual worker or of 'proletarian origin.'

As a result, managers and Party officials often approached plant problems differently. And although both aimed to serve the State's economic interests, their opinions about concrete measures often differed. The statement issued by the Central Committee of the Party in September 1929, on 'industrial management and one-man control,' [29] tried to adjust these differences according to the experiences of the NEP period: the cell was to execute 'general directives' of the Party and not to interfere in 'details' of the managers' current work, such as hiring administrative personnel, or assigning tasks to workers. For years this was the formal doctrine. But in practice it was difficult to draw a precise line between 'general directives' and 'details.'

It might be supposed that in a State consciously built as a Party dictatorship, this uncertainty would work in favor of Party officials. Yet the dominant trend in the first half of the thirties was a strengthening of the authority of economic officials, guaranteeing them greater freedom of decisions. Thus the position of

[29] *Pravda*, 7 September 1929.

the manager compared with that of the primary Party organization grew stronger. The outcome was not a more intensive subordination of economic officers to Party officials in the plant, but an increasing influence of industrial officials within higher Party organs. The new changes that began in the mid-thirties, much more complicated than may appear at first sight, ended with an almost complete elimination of friction between industrial and Party officials.

The changes were prepared by changes in the Party itself, a significant trend that can only be outlined here. For years, the Communist Party aimed to remain a workers' Party, such as it was in the first years of the Revolution. Its statutes attempted to guarantee its proletarian character by rendering particularly difficult the enrollment of non-manual workers. At the same time, it cultivated high esteem for the Old Bolsheviks, those who had belonged since the first years of the Revolution—better still, from the time of the illegal work preceding the Revolution.

The great purge of 1936-8, however, brought about a sharp break with this tradition, as a glance at statistics of Party membership will show. Statistics of membership in the Party have been scanty for the last decade and the most important sources for studying the Party's social structure are the reports of the Credentials Commissions of Party Congresses. A comparison of the reports of the most recent, those for the 17th (January-February 1934) and the 18th (March 1939) Congresses—that is, the Congresses just before and just after the great purge—reveal some interesting figures.[30]

At the time of the 18th Congress, there were 1,588,852 Party members (compared with 1,872,488 at the time of the 17th Congress, i.e. a loss of almost 300,000 members). Only 1.3 per cent, that is, hardly more than 20,000, had belonged to the Party since 1917, the year of the Revolution, or earlier. At the beginning of 1918, the Party had numbered 260,000 to 270,000 members, mostly

[30] The following figures are taken from the records of the 17th (pp. 302-4) and 18th (pp. 146-50) Congresses.

young people. Even taking into account the high mortality of Party members during the Civil War, it can be assumed that hardly fewer than 200,000 of these old members were alive at the beginning of 1939. But only 10 per cent of them remained in the Party.

Figures on the composition of Party Congresses reflect the same trend as Party membership figures. At the 17th Congress, 22.6 per cent of the Congress had been Party members since before 1917, and 17.7 per cent dated their membership from 1917; thus 40 per cent had belonged since before it took power. A total of 80 per cent of the delegates had been Party members since 1919 or earlier. Five years later, at the 18th Congress, only 5 per cent of the delegates had belonged to the Party since 1917 or before (2.6 per cent since 1917, 2.4 longer), and instead of 80 per cent, only 14.8 per cent dated their membership from 1919 or earlier.

Respect for Party membership dating from the heroic period was almost at an end. At the 18th Congress it was stressed that 70 per cent of all Party members had belonged only since 1929 or later, and that 43 per cent of the Congress delegates were in this group (the comparable figure for the 17th Congress was 2.6 per cent).

The report of the Credentials Commission of the 17th Congress emphasized with satisfaction that 9.3 per cent of the delegates were 'workers in production,' actual, not former, manual workers. This point had always been examined at Congresses. The 18th Congress ignored it. The prestige of the most glorified Stakhanov workers—Stakhanov, Busygin, Krivonos, Vinogradova, Likhoradov, Smetanin, Gudov, all of them Party members and some Congress delegates—did not suffice to secure this type of working-class elite any representation on the new Central Committee of 139 persons elected by the Congress (71 members and 68 alternates). It was but a logical development that the Congress changed the Party statutes and eliminated preferences previously granted industrial workers. The Communist Party is no longer one of manual workers.

At the same time,[31] the managing and technical personnel of industrial plants also changed. As early as 1936, 97 per cent of plant managers, 82 per cent of chiefs of construction, 40 per cent of chief engineers were Communists.[32] These percentages increased further. Young engineers who, since 1936, have occupied important positions in industrial administration have come increasingly to hold Party office, even leading posts. In plants, Party apparatus and general plant administration have become more and more homogeneous, both socially and psychologically. The roots of the friction between plant managers and Party secretaries in plants have died out.

Relations between manager and Party secretary have taken on a new character. On the whole, the Party apparatus inside the plant is today scarcely more than a part of the industrial administration. It has its special Party task—'mass work'—but also functions in general plant administration, as defined by the Party Conference of February 1941.[33] That Conference, in a detailed statement about 'the tasks of the Party organizations in the field of industry and transportation,'[34] ordered that the Party committees in the provinces and cities should have special secretaries for industry and transportation. Their task is 'to know the plants exactly, to visit them regularly, to be connected directly with the plant officers and the corresponding People's Commissariats, to support them in fulfilling the Party's plans and decisions concerning industry and transportation, to control systematically the fulfilment of those decisions, to reveal the defects in the work of the plants and to aim at their removal.'

This makes the provincial and city committees of the Party

[31] For details, see Chapter IX.

[32] Central Statistical Office, *U.S.S.R., The Country of Socialism* (Moscow, 1936), p. 94.

[33] See a, above.

[34] *Pravda,* 19 February 1941.

into organs of industrial control somehow ranged above the immediate plant administration. The Party cells, their representatives inside the plants, are no longer concerned with caring for the fulfilment of 'general directives,' as decreed by the statement of September 1929, but instead they must interest themselves in all 'details' of the plant work and life. The Party organization of the plant is thus enclosed in the general industrial administration as an auxiliary organ of the official control; in this activity it is strongly subordinated to the higher Party organs which are at the same time superior to the administration of the plant. In a sense, this arrangement serves as a substitute for the control of public economy by free public opinion. The problem of relations between the plant administration and Party bodies loses, through this development, its sociological complexity and becomes merely a problem of administrative technique.

III

Management and Employees

a. Trade Unions in the Plant

RELATIONS between Soviet plant management and employees can be treated as a problem of power distribution as well as of business techniques. The present section will try to establish whether and to what extent workers influence management. We shall not go into the stormy relations existing at the beginning of the Revolution, the efforts to put plant management under what was called 'workers' control' or 'workers' control of production.' This was, in effect, a political movement with objectives lying outside the plants. To a certain extent it facilitated the transfer of State power to the Bolsheviks in November 1917; thereafter it was checked and soon lost all significance. After the beginning of 1918, plant committees, the bearers of the idea of workers' control in 1917, were mere organs of the trade unions inside plants, with a sharply defined sphere of activity within which remnants of 'control of production' soon became insignificant.[1]

The problem of relations between plant management and employees arose again after a few years, quite independently of the old conflict about workers' control. In its new form it occupied the attention of leading circles for almost a decade. This time it was only a part of the general problem of one-man control, which

[1] See S. Schwarz, 'Betriebsraete und Productionskontrolle in Russland,' in *Die sozialen Probleme des Betriebes* (Berlin, 1925), ed. by Heinz Potthoff. The question is discussed in greater detail in S. Schwarz, 'Plant Committees and Trade Unions in the First Years of the Revolution,' a chapter in the forthcoming co-operative study of the Russian labor movement and social policy in the first years of the Revolution, to be published by the Hoover Library for War, Peace, and Revolution.

had played a significant role in the life of Russian industrial plants almost from the beginning of the Soviet regime. In the twenties the problem was one of overcoming conflicts between managers technically under-prepared for their posts, and qualified 'technical directors,' who, for political reasons, were subordinated to the managers. This question will be considered in detail in Chapter IX, below. By the end of the twenties, the problem had shifted to the interrelations between three factors: (1) the manager, (2) the plant committee representing employees and acting also as an organ of the trade union within the plant, and (3) the Communist Party organization within the plant.[2] The manager, the chairman of the workers' plant committee, and the secretary of the Party organization constituted a 'triangle' supposed to function as an *entente cordiale*. For a long time the relationship was not formally regulated. In practice, the center of gravity for economic questions proper lay in the manager. For questions that particularly interested the workers as wage-earners and consumers, the center of importance lay in the chairman of the workers' plant committee. The secretary of the Party organization had the task of ironing out and disposing of eventual clashes between the other two 'angles' and, above all, of seeing to it that the activity of manager and plant committee followed Party directives. The jurisdictions of the three were not rigidly defined and, in practice, there was often an inclination to regard the triangle itself as the real management, to which each of the three members was, to a certain extent, subordinate.

With the general tendency, beginning in the late twenties and outlined in the preceding chapters, to fortify the position of the manager within the plant, he became less hampered in his work by any consideration of the workers' plant committee. This development was essentially facilitated at the end of the twenties

[2] Relations between the plant manager and the Communist Party organization were discussed in Chapter II. The discussion in this chapter is limited to relations between the manager and the plant committee, considering the role of the Party organization only incidentally.

by fundamental changes in the recognized tasks and position of trade unions.

The Russian trade unions, in the course of the New Economic Policy (1921-8), developed into a unique type of movement. They remained organizations 'defending' and representing the special interests of wage-earners, but were restricted by the requirement of industrial peace and by the fact of State control of industry. They lost their character as organizations of industrial struggle. The fundamental conception determining their work was given sharp expression in the well-known 'theses' of the Central Committee of the Communist Party 'on the role and tasks of the trade unions under the New Economic Policy.' Written by Lenin and published early in 1922,[8] these constituted the credo of the Russian trade-union movement down to the end of 1928. One passage may be quoted from this comprehensive document:

State plants have been shifted to so-called business accountability. At the same time, it is urgently necessary to increase labor productivity, to abolish deficits and to assure profitability in every factory. All this, along with inevitable departmental interests and overzealousness, unavoidably brings about a certain clash of interests in questions of work conditions, between the working masses and the plant managers or the relevant government departments. With respect to socialized factories, trade unions have therefore the absolute duty to defend the interests of the workers. As far as possible they must help to raise the workers' material living conditions. To achieve this, the unions have to correct systematically errors and exaggerations committed by organs of economic administration and resulting from bureaucratic distortions in the State apparatus.

Of course, in line with older terminology, the theses went on to declare that 'the Communist Party and the Soviet government, as well as the trade unions, must openly recognize the existence and inevitability of the economic struggle,' until the time, that is, 'when electrification in industry and agriculture will uproot the

[8] *Pravda*, 17 January 1922.

small producer and the power of the market.' For the time being, this 'economic struggle' (within socialized plants) was expressly contrasted with the 'class struggle' (within private plants), and could in practice mean nothing but energetic representation of the interests of the wage-earners by peaceful means. Moreover, the phrase 'economic struggle' soon all but vanished from the vocabulary of the trade unions of the NEP period.

In 1929 the spine of this trade-union movement was broken. Almost all trade-union officials, who had in the years of the NEP developed into trade-union leaders, were purged and replaced by new men, chiefly from the Party apparatus. Most drastically affected by the purge was almost the entire leadership of the Central Trade Union Council, headed by Michael Tomski, who, on 1 June 1929, was removed. Thenceforth, any tendency to let trade unions concentrate on special labor interests was repudiated as 'opportunist' and 'trade unionist.'

The increase of production, above all by increasing labor productivity (through 'socialist competition,'[4] etc.) and by improving labor discipline, was thenceforth declared to be the main task of the trade unions. All other trade-union tasks, especially those connected with the improvement of working conditions, were subordinated thereto. As an inevitable consequence, the organs of trade unions within plants, the plant committees, largely ceded influence to plant managers, as primarily responsible for production.

In the fall of 1929, the Communist Party adopted an important resolution on industrial management and one-man control, mentioned in Chapter II.[5] For the first time it formally defined jurisdictions within the triangle. This resolution long powerfully influenced the internal structure of industrial plants. Although widely modified in practice over the course of years, it has never been formally repealed as a whole. It stressed the fact that thus

[4] See Chapters VI and VIII.

[5] *Pravda*, 7 September 1929. The date of adoption has not been publicly recorded.

far there had been no 'clear and sufficiently definite separation of the tasks and duties of the plant organs—the manager, the plant committee, and the Party cell.' 'There may still be found in plants direct intervention by Party and trade-union organs in the operational-productive work of the plant management.' Now, however, 'all reins of the administration of the plant's economic life must be concentrated in the hands of the plant manager,' and one-man control must be secured. The 'triangle' as a working committee was not mentioned at all, but the authority of manager, plant committee, and Party cell were respectively defined as follows:

1. The manager is in sole and full charge. All his 'operational-economic orders' are 'unconditionally binding' on the entire personnel, 'regardless of what posts they may occupy in Party, trade-union, or other organizations.' The manager alone shall select, promote, and remove administrative personnel, 'taking into consideration' but not being bound by 'the opinion of Party and trade-union organizations.'

2. The trade-union organ (workers' plant committee) 'represents the day-to-day needs of labor in the field of culture and living conditions as well as in economic life,' and is at the same time 'the energetic organizer of the productive initiative of the working masses.' It 'participates, especially through production conferences,[6] in the discussion of fundamental questions of production' and the like. This was not, however, to mean that it could make or even share in decisions. For relations between the manager and the committee on matters connected with production, the following rule was applicable:

> While trade-union organizations regularly receive reports of the plant management, study production data, and make proposals, they may not intervene directly in the running of the plant or endeavor in any way to replace plant management. They shall by all means help to secure one-man control, increased production, plant development, and, thereby, improvement of the material condition of the working class.

[6] See d, below.

3. The definition of the field of work of the Party cell—based on the distinction between 'general directives' and 'details'—presented obvious difficulties to the authors of the 7 September resolution, as was shown in Chapter II.

After 1929 trade unions increasingly lost importance both inside and outside plants.[7] Inside, they showed a growing tendency to treat all problems of factory life chiefly if not solely from the point of view of production.

So thoroughly did the productive point of view come to dominate the attitude of unions that it led, in some cases, to overzealousness, which endangered production itself. As a consequence, Stalin himself, at a conference of economic officials on 23 June 1931, stressed the necessity of paying more attention to the workers' standard of living in the interests of the development of industry. This speech inspired numerous expressions of 'self-criticism' in trade-union circles. For example:

> The trade unions have lost the feeling for the needs of the working masses [declared the chairman of the railroad union, Amosov, at a meeting of the presidium of the Central Trade Union Council, when the situation in the Stalingrad Tractor Works was discussed]. Trade unionists have held it to be in bad taste and perhaps even opportunist to be concerned with the living needs of the workers. The trade-union organizations of the Tractor Works have degenerated into a bad appendix of the economic organs. They have lost their trade-union face.[8]

But even concern for the living needs of the workers was advocated chiefly if not exclusively in terms of production needs. In connection with the above-mentioned presidium meeting, and with reference to experiences during the construction of the automobile plant at Gorki (Nizhni-Novgorod), the general trade-union organ, *Labor*, wrote in its editorial of 16 August 1931:

[7] This development and other problems covered in this chapter are discussed in detail in a forthcoming work by the author of this chapter, a study of labor policy in Russia from 1928 to 1941.

[8] *Labor*, 15 August 1931.

A number of trade-union organizations are today still unable to understand the political significance of the struggle for the systematic improvement of the material standard of living of the working class as a condition for the success of the upbuilding of socialism at its present stage. This misunderstanding is at the basis of the typical attitude of many trade-union organizations which pay no attention to the numerous horrible realities so fateful to the fulfilment of the industrial and financial plan.

With such an attitude, the trade unions were soon bound to lose all justification for existence as a factor in determining working conditions. And, as a matter of fact, their elimination from the machinery of hiring and from the process of fixing wages was rapidly achieved in the first half of the thirties.

b. Hiring Labor

In the second half of the twenties, the hiring of manpower proceeded on the basis of collective contracts: in principle, workers could be hired only through the employment service, in whose administration the trade unions played a powerful role. In plants, the plant committees had the right and duty to see to the enforcement of these provisions.

In 1931, however, plant managers were expressly given the right to hire 'directly without applying to the employment offices.' [9] And when, in 1933, the Commissariat for Labor was dissolved with all its organs, and part of its tasks were assigned to the trade unions, labor supply was not among those tasks. The hiring of labor for the plant has both formally and in fact come under plant management, with no vestige of union influence.

In order to stimulate the influx of manpower to the factories, an energetic policy of 'activizing urban labor reserves' was developed at the beginning of the thirties. An attempt was made to influence the working masses so that those members of the family not gainfully employed—especially housewives—would turn to

[9] Decree of the Central Executive Committee and the Council of People's Commissars, 13 September 1931, *Laws and Ordinances*, 1931:385.

wage labor. It was primarily propagandistic and was undertaken by the Communist Party, the Young Communist League, and the trade unions, although, again, the latter had no influence on actual hiring decisions in or outside the plants. The effort was materially facilitated by the unfavorable trend of real wages in the first half of the thirties.

The problem of labor procurement could not, however, be solved by hiring simply those who applied at plants. Beyond that, plants and economic organs had to undertake an energetic recruitment campaign, particularly among the rural population. For this purpose a special organization was created which found definite shape in the decree of 21 July 1938. This decree set up a central commission for regulating organized recruiting of manpower, and similar commissions for constituent Republics and for the several provinces. For the U.S.S.R. and the constituent Republics, the commissions include the Vice-Chairman of the Council of People's Commissars, the People's Commissar for Agriculture, and the Chairman of the State Planning Commission. Thus the commissions are primarily interdepartmental organs, designed to co-ordinate the work of organs concerned with current procurement of manpower.

The central commission, on the basis of data provided by the economic Commissariats, established the total number of workers to be obtained from rural areas and set quotas for the various constituent Republics and provinces. Within these quotas, the provinces were ordered by the central commission to procure manpower for particular economic Commissariats whenever necessary. As a rule, one province could be called upon by only one Commissariat—i.e. by one industry—in exceptional cases, by two or three. In such cases the districts within a province would be assigned to Commissariats by the provincial commission, so that Commissariats would not compete with each other in the procurement of labor power. The Commissariats, the trusts subordinate to them, and even individual large plants sent into their assigned provinces fully authorized agents equipped with small staffs, to operate with the support of local Soviets and kolkhoz committees. Trade unions have no part in these activities.

c. Fixing Wages and Labor Conditions

The influence of trade unions and of workers' plant committees on fixing wages and labor conditions was important until the end of the twenties, but vanished gradually as collective contracts first ceased to be an instrument of labor policy and then died away.

In the twenties all collective contracts in the Soviet Union were renewed annually, at about the same time of year in all branches of industry, through an organized drive conducted by the economic authorities and the trade unions. When opening the annual drive in the fall of 1929, the Central Trade Union Council and the Supreme Economic Council urged the economic organs and trade unions to conduct the drive as 'a broad campaign with economic aims.' They were 'to concentrate the attention of the working class on concrete economic tasks,' i.e. 'increase of labor productivity, strengthening labor discipline, lowering production costs, improvement of production quality, mobilization of industry's inner resources, implementing the continuous labor week, etc.' [10]

The transformation of the collective contract into an instrument of economic policy for improvement of production, which only indirectly would improve labor's standards of living, soon led to the question whether collective contracts were at all necessary. Although maintained in form in the early thirties, they dealt more and more exclusively with norms of performance, labor discipline, technical improvements, etc. Beginning with the spring of 1933, no collective contract could go beyond existing legislative provisions for labor protection.[11] At the end of 1933, col-

[10] *Pravda,* 29 September 1929.

[11] Joint ordinance of the Central Trade Union Council and the several economic People's Commissariats, 4 March 1933. *For Industrialization,* 5 March 1933; and *Soviet Labor Law,* textbook published by the People's Commissariat for Justice (Moscow, 1939), pp. 60-61.

lective contracts were not renewed. Those written for 1933 were generally continued for 1934 and a few were written for 1935. Since then no collective contracts have been written or renewed.[12] As collective contracts died away, trade unions and plant committees gradually ceased to participate in fixing wages in the plant.

Fixing of wage rates in the Soviet Union has been, almost from the beginning, a dual process: (a) the setting-up of a schedule of relative wage rates, expressed as multiples of the wage rate of the lowest-paid category of workers; and (b) the fixing of this lowest wage rate generally on a monthly, sometimes on a weekly or daily basis. Both elements were present in the collective contracts. As collective contracts gradually died away, wage-fixing machinery became somewhat indefinite. The old schedules of relative wage rates were taken over; the fixing of wage rates of the lowest category (which determines all others) became, in fact, a function of the various organs of industrial management (plant manager or higher bodies), who had to keep within the pay-roll allowances fixed by the Plan.[13] Occasionally they also revised the schedules of relative rates; since 1938 [14] these schedules have been set up by the People's Commissariats and approved by the Economsoviet.

Piece rates—the prevailing form of pay—are usually fixed in Russia separately for each plant. The piece rates are determined by two factors: a monthly wage rate fixed as described above, and the performance norm fixed, as a rule, for the individual plant. The piece rate equals time rate divided by performance norm.

Participation in determining the performance norm had, for years, been one of the most important tasks of labor's representatives within the plant. The 1922 Labor Code, still formally valid, expressly provides that 'performance norms shall be determined by the plant management and trade union or the corresponding trade-union organ' (Art. 56). Accordingly, special bodies were

[12] *Soviet Labor Law*, p. 61.
[13] See Chapter IV.
[14] *Laws and Ordinances*, 1938:178.

organized in the plant on a parity basis, the Piece-Rates and Conflicts Committees (RKK, *Rastzenochno-Konfliktnyye Komissii*). If these committees reached no agreement, the performance norms were submitted to a conciliation body, also an inner-plant organ. Labor's representatives in both bodies were named by the plant committee.

During the thirties, however, the Piece-Rates Committees gradually lost power to pure organs of the plant administration, the bureaus for wages and norms. Since 1933 these bureaus have had exclusive jurisdiction in fixing performance norms.[15] Only when these are obviously 'wrong' may the Piece-Rates Committee, on the initiative of its labor members, suggest revision. The labor members of the Piece-Rates Committee have, in addition, the task of popularizing among workers the norms and rates fixed by management, and holding labor up to fulfilment of the norms.

Inevitably the workers' plant committees lost their important functions. This is particularly true of the protection of labor, a field with which plant committees legally are supposed to be concerned. Through 'labor inspectors,' who are nominated by them from among workers and elected by workers, plant committees are supposed to supervise the carrying out of labor legislation. Plant committees can make proposals to management, give or withhold consent to certain suspensions of statutory provisions (e.g. with respect to overtime), etc. But such recommendations or protests have often been disregarded. For example: In an Astrakhan cannery there were disagreements between Plant Director Krutzov and Plant Committee Chairman Suslin. Suslin

demanded that Krutzov make no changes concerning the day off without his consent. He further demanded that Krutzov refund to the workers 12,000 roubles which had been collected for agricultural work[16] but which had not been spent . . . Comrade

[15] Resolution of the presidium of the Central Trade Union Council of 2 January 1933. Published in *Labor*, 9 May 1933.

[16] To finance a farm producing food for the plant workers. The entire quotation is from *Labor*, 22 April 1934.

Suslin tried verbally to resolve the differences with the Director, but since he got nowhere he declined to submit his demands to the Director in writing, which, of course, was a mistake.

The Director pulled all the wires and the presidium of the Astrakhan Trade Union Council replaced Suslin with another trade unionist. But:

when the Director learned who had been named chairman of the plant committee, he declared: 'I won't accept him. I won't allow any multiple government in my plant. We don't need any outsider. I recommend another comrade.' And the municipal Trade Union Council confirmed Krutzov's candidate.

Of course, this case is crude in form. But five or ten years earlier, no such case could have been conceived.[17] To be sure, even in later times, labor unions have been occasionally declared to be 'lower organs of State auditing in the plant.' [18] In practice, this meant they were merely watching over food supplied by factory farms and canteens, sometimes supervising factory crèches and hospitals, etc.[19]

This was the course that the Russian trade-union movement took eventually—with slight vacillations, to be sure, and, in the first years, against some opposition from workers and trade-union officers.

Thus, one member of the 'triangle' gradually dwindled into total insignificance. And thereby the fate of the whole triangle was sealed. Early in 1937 it was openly declared that the triangle had no more justification for existing. In the plenary session of the Central Committee, Zhdanov declared:

[17] Material on this question is contained in the author's articles in the Russian fortnightly, *Socialist Courier* (Paris, now New York): 'The Dying out of the Trade Unions' (1934, No. 9); 'Significant Polemics between the Trade Union Press and the Economic Press' (1935, No. 11); 'The Crisis of Labor Protection' (1937, Nos. 11, 12-13); 'The Thorny Path of Labor Protection' (1938, No. 20-21).

[18] 17th Party Congress, p. 673. The official designation of State auditing agencies is 'workers' and peasants' comptrollership.'

[19] *Soviet Justice* (1934), No. 23, p. 18; No. 28, p. 22.

From the standpoint of correct relations between the Party, the economic organs and the trade-union organs, the triangle is something quite impermissible . . . The triangle is a sort of administrative board, but our economic administration is constructed along totally different lines.[20]

Thereafter, nothing further was heard about the triangle.

d. Workers' 'Production Conferences'

While the influence of labor unions in the plant diminished, one field was kept open for workers' initiative and action: they were encouraged to organize 'conferences on production,' whose origin goes back to about 1924. The 14th Party Congress (1925), while urging a fight against 'errors and deviations' of such conferences towards 'direct administration and management of enterprises,' recognized their educational value:

Production conferences in factories, plants and other large enterprises and economic units are the best way of drawing the working masses into the task of the practical construction of Soviet economy; of fostering in them a realization of the close tie between the interests of the toilers and the degree of economic success of the socialist state; and of selecting and educating new contingents of economic officials and administrators of working class origin.[21]

These conferences are not composed of representatives, but of individual employees interested in production matters, who attend on their own initiative or are invited by the organizers. Since the beginning of the Stakhanov movement (1935), the Stakhanovites, members of shock brigades,[22] foremen, and technical personnel, have been the mainstays of production conferences. Formally, the conferences are led by workers' plant committees, but in reality their organization and scope, never defined precisely, vary from

[20] *Pravda*, 11 March 1937.

[21] 14th Party Congress, p. 979.

[22] The shock brigaders (*udarniki*) are those workers who achieve record performances. Performances of Stakhanovites are still higher; Stakhanovites presumably have introduced new methods of intensive and planned work.

plant to plant and from time to time, as does their influence on the life of the plant.

In one section of the huge Magnitogorsk works (Ural), the production conference meets twice a month to hear reports of the section head on progress in fulfilling the monthly plan, and to discuss fundamental or topical problems of production. It is claimed that many valuable suggestions have been made by workers at these conferences and quickly carried out. In another large Ural metallurgical factory, asserts a correspondent of *Stakhanovetz,* shortcomings in the work of a section were eliminated as a result of suggestions made by workers at a production conference.[23]

A vivid picture of the functioning of the workers' 'collective' in a large Moscow tannery is given by *Stakhanovetz.*[24] The workers decided at an open meeting to fulfil in four years the official 'five year plan for raising the productivity of labor.' The management accepted the suggestion, promised to study possibilities and to work out technological and administrative measures. 'Such a plan could be worked out only if Stakhanovites, shock brigaders, engineers, and technicians would take an active part in its formulation.' A committee consisting of the chairman of the plant committee and its wage commission, the chief engineer, assistant engineer, and the head of the department of technical supervision, organized seven study groups to deal with utilization of waste, transport, skilled labor, experiences of Stakhanovites, etc. Two hundred men were elected to the study groups at production conferences of individual sections of the plant. The study groups were aided by Stakhanovites, inventors, etc. They discussed problems with the personnel of relevant sections and workshops, gathered material on workers' inventions, waste, unused reserves, etc. When this work was finished, a large 'Stakhanovite tech-

[23] *The Stakhanovite* (1940), No. 7, p. 39, discussions at a conference (mainly of Stakhanovites and engineers) summoned by the Central Trade Union Council in May 1940.

[24] Ibid. (1940), No. 12, pp. 23ff.

nological conference' was summoned, in which all members of the study groups and many engineers and plant officials took part. This conference submitted to the management a plan for raising labor productivity. The plan and all underlying material were carefully studied by a special commission of the management. Finally the plan was adopted and carried out.

IV

The Planning of Industrial Production

IN principle at least, all economic activity in the U.S.S.R. is directed along lines laid down by the government and the Communist Party in a Plan, one part of which is devoted to industry. 'Directives' and norms laid down in the Five Year Plan and in annual and quarterly plans determine the functioning of industry as a whole, as well as of its individual branches and single plants. The highest planning body is the *Gosplan* (State Planning Commission) of the U.S.S.R.

a. THE GOSPLAN

The Gosplan was created in 1921.[1] Since that time it has often been reorganized, and its functions and authority within the system of supreme Soviet organs have been altered. It now operates in conformity with the Gosplan Statutes of 1938, as amended;[2] it consists of 54 departments and employs about 1,000 planning officials.

The Gosplan receives from the Central Committee of the Communist Party and the Council of People's Commissars general directives on which to base Five Year, annual, and quarterly plans. Starting from these, it draws up plans for the various sectors of economic activity (heavy industry, light industry, transport, agriculture, etc.) and for the various territorial regions. It amalga-

[1] Decree of 22 February 1921, in *Laws and Ordinances*, 1921:106; reprinted on the twentieth anniversary of Gosplan in *Planned Economy* (1941), No. 2, pp. 5-6.

[2] Decrees of 2 February 1938 and 31 December 1941, in *Laws and Ordinances*, 1938:41, and 1941:27.

mates such partial plans into a single Plan, which it submits to the Council of People's Commissars of the U.S.S.R. for approval. The Gosplan not only draws plans, but also supervises fulfilment by People's Commissariats and single plants. The Gosplan Statutes set as its main task 'securing proper proportions in the development of various fields and preventing disproportions in economic activity.'

Moreover, the Gosplan may submit to the Council of People's Commissars or to the Central Committee of the Party, special economic plans and projects of fundamental importance. Before the final approval of the first Five Year Plan, the Gosplan had worked out and submitted to the Central Committee five or six preliminary drafts, which were rejected as not conforming to Party policy. More recently, especially since the purges of 1937-8, the Gosplan has shown little initiative and usually awaits Party directives.

The so-called 'functional' departments of the Gosplan lay out plans for the erection of new factories and works. They determine production figures, requirements of raw materials and man power, and financial needs. About twenty other departments, roughly corresponding to as many industrial People's Commissariats, are engaged in planning and supervising individual branches of industry and are called 'production' departments, e.g. the departments of ferrous metallurgy, machine-building, etc. Other departments elaborate, relate, and supervise plans for various regions.[3]

Attached to the Gosplan since 1938[4] are 'chief Gosplan delegates' for regions or large plants, who supervise fulfilment on the spot and may alter plans when necessary.

The distinction originally sought, between 'functional' departments for particular problems common to all industries, and 'production' departments specializing in individual industries, has never materialized. It has proved impossible to draw a strict line

[3] See c, below.
[4] Decree of 2 February 1938, loc. cit.

of demarcation: 'functional' and 'production' departments must constantly adapt themselves to each other. When, for example, a new Ural metallurgical plant is being planned, the following Gosplan departments must reach an agreement: the (functional) departments for transport, finances, etc.; the (production) departments for metallurgy and construction. In this case, either the Gosplan department for metallurgy or that for construction—or the regional main delegate of the Gosplan—would supervise construction.

Economic planning for each constituent Republic is headed by a separate Gosplan. The Gosplan of the Ukraine, for example, is formally that Republic's highest planning organ, although actually it functions more like a regional organ of the Gosplan of the U.S.S.R. The Gosplan of the various Republics carry out general directives of the central Gosplan. In addition, they direct research on local natural resources and economic potentialities, publish economic periodicals, etc. We shall return to these organs in dealing with regional planning.

b. Intermediate Planning Organs

The general planning directives of the Gosplan, approved by the Council of People's Commissars, are carried out by People's Commissariats and Glavks. Except where more than one People's Commissariat is concerned (as in the production of electric power or of building materials, plans for which are worked out by the Gosplan itself), the planning department of a People's Commissariat works out a plan for its branch of industry and gives directives to the largest plants (others receive theirs through Glavks or Trusts).

The planning department of a Glavk functions analogously to a People's Commissariat planning department. Its directives to plants in its special branch (e.g. making of machine tools, a branch of machine building) are naturally more detailed and concrete than those of higher agencies. In particular, the Glavk planning department allocates production to single plants and settles interrelations among plants jointly producing certain goods.

During the early years of planning (first and second Five Year Plans), production plans paid closest attention to the construction of new plants, or to defining production programs of plants nearing completion. Plants producing automobiles were shifted to tractors; machine construction works changed types of products; etc. The efficiency and capacity of the newly built plants were not yet tested.

At that time, almost every plan had to do considerable traveling before obtaining final approval. The original directives would move from Gosplan down to the plant, passing through all economic agencies (People's Commissariat, Glavk, Trust). There would follow a return journey: plant and lower agencies would check original suggestions and send them on up to Gosplan. The latter would then co-ordinate the suggestions of various plants and transmit final orders to individual plants via the intermediary agencies. Today such voyages are faster and often shorter, owing to the experience accumulated at all levels of planning and in production itself.

Many plants have been given the initiative in working out their own production programs in line with directives of the previous year, without waiting for new orders from above; they transmit their programs to the Glavk or directly to the People's Commissariat. The Glavk checks and, if necessary, changes plans, taking into account supply possibilities unknown to the plant, the possibility of co-operation between plants, financial resources, regional needs, etc. The Glavk draws up a consolidated program for the aggregate of its subordinate plants, which is checked and, if necessary, changed by the People's Commissariat. Lastly, the Gosplan carries out similar co-ordination for all Soviet industry, producing an annual Plan, passed along as a 'directive' through all agencies down to the plants. Thus the first part of the triple journey is now often dropped. In the case of new industries or new plants not firmly established, however, planning begins as before with Gosplan directives, and every plan makes the triple journey. Quarterly planning procedure is simpler, as it does not need the approval of any agency higher than a Glavk.

c. Regional Planning

During the first Five Year Plan, Gosplan as well as the People's Commissariats gave their main attention to planning by industrial divisions, with regional planning subordinated. The second Five Year Plan was more conscious of the importance of planning territorial distribution of industry than was the first. The necessity of moving manufacturing nearer to sources of fuel and raw materials, the interests of the 'autonomous national Republics,' and strategic considerations were more fully recognized. Plans for the territorial distribution of industry were, however, laid out mainly by central organs: the Gosplan, People's Commissariats, Glavks. The part played by regional planning organs was rather insignificant.[5]

The Gosplan Statutes of 2 February 1938 showed the importance attached by Soviet leaders to regional planning. The 18th Party Congress (Resolution on the third Five Year Plan) emphasized the necessity of 'bringing industry nearer to sources of raw materials and centers of consumption. This will both shorten transportation distances, and develop economically backward areas . . . The Plan provides for further economic and cultural advance of the autonomous national Republics and of provinces.'[6]

To the two relevant departments of Gosplan—'Regional Planning' and 'Geographic Distribution of Plants'—nine territorial departments were added when it was reorganized in 1940. Until this recent reorganization, the functions of regional and local planning committees (attached to the highest executive organs of regions)

[5] 'In working out the plan for the development of individual regions during the second Five Year Plan, Gosplan leaned on the work of local planning committees, the studies of the narkomats and research institutes. Gosplan, *Draft of the Second Five Year Plan* (Moscow, 1934), II:5.

[6] 18th Party Congress, p. 660.

were somewhat nominal. They confined themselves, in the main, to 'applications' (*zayavka*) for funds to carry out local plans. These applications seem frequently to have been a method of pressure of sectional interests on central planning bodies. Such 'applications' were reckoned with in shaping final plans, although central planning bodies were inclined to discount many of them.[7]

In the spring of 1937, the Chairman of the Planning Committee of the Russian Republic, S. Karp, complained about poor connections among that Republic's planning organs.[8] Identical complaints were published late in 1940.[9] The declared intention of considering local needs and granting more power to local organs is in harmony with the tendency of enhancing the plant managers' initiative. The government probably understood that an eventual war would disrupt supply and transport. It sought to relax to a certain degree centralized planning and management, especially for local industry working mainly for local consumption.

At the beginning of 1941, the Council of People's Commissars and the Central Committee of the Party issued a decree intended to decentralize, for plants of local importance, planning, financing, supply of raw materials, and disposal of products. In particular, almost all planning of production and sale of consumption goods by local industries and handicraft co-operatives (artels) was transferred to local authorities. Central boards for the supervision of handicraft co-operatives were abolished.[10]

[7] Many instances of exaggerated applications from local 'planners' can be found in the Gosplan's official review, *The Plan*, especially for 1937 (Nos. 8-10). For later instances, see also A. Korobov, 'Tasks of Complex Regional Planning,' in *Planned Economy* (1940), No. 11, pp. 39-46.

[8] *The Plan* (1937), No. 8, p. 30.

[9] 'One of the causes of poor supervision of Plan fulfilment is the weak connection between local planning committees and the Gosplans of the constituent Republics, and the inadequate supervision of these committees by the Gosplan of the U.S.S.R.' See A. Korobov, op. cit. p. 45.

[10] Decree of 7 January 1941, on 'Measures for Increasing the Production of Goods for Mass Consumption and Food out of Local Raw Materials,' *Laws and Ordinances*, 1941:40.

d. Plant Planning

S. M. Kirov, one of the most vigorous Soviet economic leaders, characterized as 'a real piece of socialism' the *tekhpromfinplan* of a plant (i.e. its technical, industrial and financial plan), and Molotov, at the 17th Party Congress, praised planning by single plants as 'one of the best socialist methods of struggle for our tempo.' [11] As a matter of fact, this element of the Soviet planning machinery is in many ways quite similar to the planning of production by the individual capitalist entrepreneur.

On the level of a single plant the impulse to planning is given by directives issued by a People's Commissariat or Glavk directly or, if the plant belongs to one, by a Trust. 'Directives' cover: (1) approximate production in quantity and money value; (2) volume and kind of new capital investment; (3) amount of working capital; (4) number of workers and desired increase in labor efficiency; (5) 'wages fund' (annual pay roll) and planned increase in average earnings; (6) planned reduction in the cost of production; and (7) planned reduction per unit of product in the use of fuel, electric power, and raw materials.

Next, these directives must be adjusted in detail to the plant's concrete technical potential. The result is the plant 'production program,' worked out by the plant management; in large plants it is based on departmentalized 'operative programs.' Active participation of engineers and workers in the formulation of programs is encouraged.[12] As a rule, plant management is supposed to specify qualities and quantities of particular commodities to be produced for sale or internal use, keeping within the figure of aggregate output (and, sometimes, output of main product) set in the directives. Management may, however, propose to higher agencies a change in the aggregate figure. At one time, so-called 'counter-plans,' usually instigated by the Communist organization in the plant or by Stakhanovites, were common: a

[11] i.e. for speed in production.
[12] See Chapter III.d.

plant management would ask a higher agency to revise its assignment upward.

Further elaboration transforms a 'production program' into a plant tekhpromfinplan. Subject to approval by higher agencies whenever their directives are transgressed, there are added to production figures (1) an estimate of the required number of workers; (2) an estimate of pay roll; (3) a plan for lowering cost of production; (4) an estimate of fuel, electric power, raw materials, semi-finished products, and equipment to be acquired; (5) a plan for utilizing plant equipment; (6) proposed organizational and technological measures for the best utilization of all plant resources (*orgtekhplan*); and finally, (7) the financial plan, i.e. a balance-sheet to be aimed at by the management.

Other important items usual in a tekhpromfinplan are distribution of products, introduction of new processes, auxiliary production, details of capital investment (expansion), co-operation with other plants. The People's Commissariat or Glavk issues general directives for co-operation among plants, indicating in particular those plants which might deliver needed semi-finished goods or machine parts, those which might need certain products. A plant producing motors would, for example, be informed both about potential supplies of iron castings and about motor requirements of agricultural-machine factories. Such recommendations are supposed to form the basis of a detailed plan of co-operation, worked out by plant management and covering specifications, prices, and delivery dates. Such a plan must be approved by higher agencies, which thereupon work out official 'co-operation agreements' between plants.

When the tekhpromfinplan is finally approved by the higher authorities, it becomes law for the plant management. As a matter of fact, however, the plant plan, like those of other economic agencies, including that of Gosplan itself, is subject to repeated changes in process of application, because of changes in general economic conditions or alterations in Party policy.

e. From Plan to Reality

The most obvious feature of Soviet plant management is the fact that it must act within the framework of a general Plan. Capitalist management, too, must reckon with a general framework of legal institutions, a given supply and demand, etc. But even if no capitalist plant works in a vacuum, the manager of a capitalist plant has wide latitude in choosing his course; he is bound to no established plan of production, supply, and delivery. The Soviet manager, on the contrary, must carry out strict instructions issued by the higher organs of State and Party. 'The economic life of the U.S.S.R. is determined and guided,' says Article 11 of the Constitution of the U.S.S.R., 'by an economic plan of development elaborated by the State . . .' The aims of the Plan are derived from political conceptions of the Communist Party. No deviation from the 'general line' of Party policy is allowed. Only in later years has economic practice become somewhat more elastic. After a period of 'Plan fetishism,' an inclination to regard a Plan as 'something dynamic' is observable.

As early as the period when the first Five Year Plan was worked out, Stalin coined the slogan: 'Our Plans are neither predictions nor conjectures; they are directives.'[13] The first 'directives' were inspired by the idea of rapid industrialization. As early as the 16th Party Congress (1930), Stalin scorned 'bureaucrats who can believe that the work of planning is finished when a plan has been drawn. The elaboration of a plan is only the beginning of planning. The real planning work develops only afterwards, after control is carried out on the spot [mainly by Party organizations], in the process of applying and correcting the plan and of making the plan more precise.'[14] When the 18th Party Congress (1939) ordered that planning be reorganized, it urged in particular the necessity of current 'check-ups on fulfilment of plans'; 'the actual

[13] 15th Party Congress, p. 69.
[14] 16th Party Congress, p. 49.

results achieved must dictate the necessary amendments to plans, whether for individual industries or regions.' [15]

During the period of the third Five Year Plan, and especially in 1940, the idea of continual check-ups and re-adjustments of plans gained ground. Leaders of Soviet planning came to the conclusion that 'we have not as yet achieved a real economic plan and a full guarantee of its fulfilment.' [16] 'Our planning,' complained L. Meizenberg, an outstanding planning official, 'is still to a great extent clerical and statistical work, absolutely divorced from economic practice . . .' [17]

In a decision of 8 February 1940, Gosplan condemned the old methods of mere 'bureaucratic-statistical methods of planning,' and recommended 'the reshaping of planning work in the direction of real control of the fulfilment of plan.' [18] According to this decision, it seems that Gosplan now has the responsibility not only of drawing up plans but also of adjusting them. In principle, it has always been that way, but in practice there has been 'in the minds of planning workers the idea that planning organs are responsible only for drawing up plans and not for their further course and results.' [19] Planning officials sometimes are inclined to 'pin themselves to figures.' [20]

In its decision of 8 February 1940, Gosplan pointed out that failure to fulfil a plan is often due not only to defects in the work of the narkomats, but to blunders in planning. Gosplan, therefore, recommended a series of measures to guarantee fulfilment by constant supervision of all economic life. Planning officials were urged to work out measures to safeguard for the current year (1940) the planned output of locomotives and wagons; to put an end to cross-hauling and other faults in the work of railways, etc.

[15] 18th Party Congress, p. 665.
[16] Decree of 16 April 1940; *Pravda*, 18 April 1940.
[17] 'On the Economic Plan,' in *Planned Economy* (1940), No. 10, p. 12.
[18] *Planned Economy* (1940), No. 2, pp. 120-21.
[19] Editorial, 'For the Further Improvement of Planning,' in *Planned Economy* (1940), No. 3, p. 27.
[20] *Planned Economy* (1940), No. 10, p. 26.

In the most important Gosplan departments, special assistant chiefs have been appointed to supervise fulfilment of plan in particular branches of industry. At the same time, the established function of the 'chief delegates' of Gosplan attained new significance.

The practice of planning has gradually brought the leaders of Soviet economy to the conclusion that tasks set by Plan must be adjusted in accordance with practice, that planning cannot be confined to orders but requires continual checking in every phase of production. In theory, these rules were formulated unequivocally, long ago. As a matter of fact, principles were not applied until the outbreak of war in the summer of 1941.

V

Procurement and Sale

a. Organization

THE requirements of individual regions and industries are laid down in an annual procurement Plan worked out by Gosplan and subject to the approval of the Economsoviet.[1] The allocation of raw materials and other producers' goods to industrial plants is thus subject to the control of government agencies. Degrees of control and centralization vary, however. Economic legislation and practice classify producers' goods into three large groups: (1) 'funded' commodities; (2) those allocated in quotas ('contingents'); (3) those supplied in 'decentralized' manner.

'Funded' commodities may not be disposed of by agencies producing them (plants, Glavks, or People's Commissariats); they are distributed to the users (People's Commissariats, Glavks, Trusts, plants, scientific institutes) by direct order of the Economsoviet, in quantities and for purposes fixed in advance by Plan. This group of commodities includes the most important producers' goods, about 300 items in all, including raw materials, fuel, machines and other equipment, motor vehicles, etc. To make the best possible use of the generally limited supply of such essential goods, the government undertakes their distribution to individual users for specified uses.

A 'quota commodity' is supplied by the People's Commissariat of the producing industry to any individual user, provided the aggregate quota allotted to the user's industry or region in the procurement plan is not exhausted. Purposes are not specified in

[1] See Chapters I and IV.

advance. Commodities in this group, while also scarce, are less urgently essential than the 'funded' ones to plants or ultimate consumers. They include, for example, timber, glass for chemistry equipment, electric fans and irons, petroleum, matches, etc.

The main commodities of the third group are scarce products of agriculture that are used industrially, and products of local handicrafts and industries (including, in particular, certain local building materials). These are subject to 'decentralized' supply.

As needs and available supplies change from year to year, the Economsoviet reclassifies annually and publishes revised lists of funded and quota commodities. Funded production is not put on the market. Quota production, to the extent destined for ultimate consumers, is offered for sale in stores, within regional quotas. Decentralized products are sold in State and co-operative stores as well as in public markets, and direct sales by producers are permitted. Sales are made on the basis of wholesale or retail prices. Transactions between government agencies or plants do not, as a rule, require cash payments.[2]

Each industrial People's Commissariat has a Main Procurement Board (*Glavsnab*) to provide plants with funded and quota commodities.[3] The Board determines the requirements of each plant and draws up annual and quarterly procurement plans, subject to the approval of the central planning and regulating bodies (Gosplan and Economsoviet); it distributes stocks allotted to a People's Commissariat among the latter's constituent Glavks and largest plants; it mobilizes all resources available at the People's Commissariat and not utilized in plants. Together with the Glavks, the Main Procurement Board of a People's Commissariat works out norms of utilization of raw materials, fuel, etc., and sends inspectors to supervise plants and insure rational fuel utilization.

For each important kind of material required by an industry, a Main Procurement Board has, as a rule, special cost-accounting

[2] See Chapter VII.

[3] P. A. Stein, *Organization of the Supply of Materials of a Socialist Industrial Plant* (Moscow, 1939), pp. 10-13.

offices and Procurement Trusts. Non-ferrous metallurgy, for example, has attached to its Main Procurement Board a Procurement Trust of chemical raw materials, another for equipment, etc. The Main Procurement Board or its Trusts have scattered local offices. On the whole, the Procurement Trusts perform current operations, leaving to other organs of the Main Board the setting up of supply plans and norms.

On a lower administrative level, the procurement department of each Glavk receives goods from its People's Commissariat's Main Procurement Board and distributes them among plants (except the largest ones). It is also responsible for periodical plant planning of prospective requirements and submits such plans to the Main Procurement Board.

To obtain funded or quota goods, a user must receive from the relevant procurement organ a voucher ordering either the warehouse of the procurement organ or the producing plant to deliver a given quantity of goods. Vouchers are issued within the framework of an agreement between a producer and a user—of which more presently. The costs of loading and shipping are paid by the supplying organ or plant, or by the user, depending on the agreement. Procurement organs have developed extensive warehousing of their own, although the legislation intended direct transportation of goods from plant to plant. Storage by procurement organs had been visualized as exceptional, and this practice, as well as extensive movement of goods from one agency to another, has been much criticized. The high cost of warehouse operations (about 30 per cent) in relation to the total turnover value of procurement organs is viewed with alarm.

Procurement for decentralized commodities is less rigid. The individual plant obtains the goods directly, mainly from such neighborhood sources as local plants, artels, and kolkhozes. This part of a plant's requirements is often very important.

As a counterpart of procurement organizations, People's Commissariats and Glavks have Sales Boards (*Glavsbyt*) to dispose of products intended for further use in production.

Consumers' goods made in industrial plants may be sold directly in specialized retail stores of plants or trusts. They may be taken over by the People's Commissariat for Supply [4] and sold in its stores. They may be transmitted to the Central Consumers' Co-operative, which distributes in villages. Under prevailing conditions of scarcity, the work of sales boards is naturally beset with fewer difficulties, administrative and otherwise, than the work on the purchasing side.

Procurement operations are based on agreements [5] concluded between buying and selling bodies, whether agencies of a People's Commissariat (or Glavks), or individual plants, after procurement plans have been approved. The earlier, centralized method of 'general agreements' between People's Commissariats (or Glavks) through their selling and buying agencies (i.e. Sales Boards and Procurement Boards) has been more and more superseded by decentralized, so-called 'direct agreements.' The former general agreements specified in considerable detail conditions of supply for a whole period, allowing plants to determine only individual deliveries. In a direct agreement, plants concerned are free to fix all conditions of supply, provided these fit approved plans and are expressly approved by higher agencies. Direct agreements may be concluded, in particular, in cases of decentralized goods or special equipment, or where constant economic interrelations exist between the producing and the consuming plant. Recently such cases seem to have been interpreted liberally enough to make centralized, general agreements infrequent and direct agreements a rule, at least for large plants.

[4] See Chapter I.

[5] Decree of 19 December 1933, in *Laws and Ordinances*, 1933:73. Each year the Economsoviet prepares a decree on a similar pattern, setting forth deficiencies of preceding 'campaigns' for concluding agreements. For specimens of general and local agreements, see L. Ginzburg and others, *Soviet Economic Legislation* (Moscow, 1934), II:47-53.

b. The Role of Management in Procurement and Sale

Since procurement is both planned and executed by higher organs, the role of the plant manager in this field is somewhat peculiar. He seems to lack all opportunity for action and still to be responsible for results, i.e. output. In theory, higher agencies must supply plants with all necessary fuel, raw materials, semi-finished goods and equipment, and organize the sale of finished products. In practice, however, the plant manager must watch carefully lest the procurement plan not be carried out in time. To obtain goods, he must often send representatives to supplying factories or to agencies of People's Commissariats and Glavks. Many plants have permanent representatives in Moscow or other supply centers with the special task of securing the timely supply of goods, of 'pushing' orders for materials, of arranging shipments, etc. And, of course, the plant management must maintain a storage organization.

A plant manager who does not get needed goods in time is often compelled to break rules and seek new ways of supplying his plant. There is thus a contradiction between theory and practice. Theory has, recently, taken a few steps toward practice, e.g. the 'direct agreements.'

Selling is far easier. The manager sells his funded and quota products through higher selling organs. For goods of the decentralized category, above all goods destined for ultimate consumption, he must study consumer needs, take the initiative, find buyers. Owing to the scarcity of commodities, however, Soviet producers are faced with no acute problem in finding a market.

c. Critical Voices

The economic literature and general press of the Soviet Union severely criticize the supply system, charging cumbrousness and inefficiency. An article published at the end of the second Five Year Plan by two planning officials described supply of industrial plants as ill-organized, and relations between producing and consuming plants as far from normal; 'despite the reiterated instructions of Party and government . . . this important section of the economic front remains one of the most backward . . . People's Commissariats and Glavks are badly informed as to the real needs of the various branches of industry for raw materials, fuel and equipment.' [6] The specialized daily press of the period frequently reported failures of the supply system.

On 3 June 1938, the Council of People's Commissars issued a decree concentrating sale of ferrous metals in a new board. Some six months later, the head of this board, S. Volikov, complained about 'individualistic methods' of procuring metals. Metals were sent from one end of the Union to the other without reason or plan. Often large quantities were brought from the Urals or Krivoi Rog (Ukraine) to Moscow as a storage and supply center, only to retrace a portion of the original route to get to a consumer.[7]

Cross-hauling is only one undesirable result. The turnover of many supply organizations, particularly local offices, is so insignificant that they are compelled to transgress their jurisdiction to justify their existence. They buy materials and equipment not needed in their own branch of industry and sell to plants of other branches. They become, in a sense, ordinary dealers.

If numerous public complaints of managers can be accepted as true, the supply even of the largest plants seems still inadequate. Commodity funds (stocks) are often apportioned only five to six days before the beginning of a quarter; 'realization' (delivery) is sometimes greatly delayed. Ordinarily, delivery is obtained only towards the end of a quarter, say in its last three or four weeks. The amount of goods apportioned for a quarter is almost always below a plant's real needs, because the People's

[6] Gaposhkin and Abakumov, 'On Procurement of Raw Materials and Equipment,' in *Planned Economy* (1938), No. 11, pp. 100-108.

[7] S. Volikov, 'On Superfluous Links in Metal Supply,' *Industry*, 31 December 1938. Analogous facts and criticisms are found in J. Gorfinkel, 'On Planning the Distribution of Metals,' *Industry*, 11 June 1938.

Commissariat and Glavk usually fear that the manager's application for goods, especially scarce materials, is exaggerated.

Another fault of the supply system is inadequate co-operation between large and small plants. The now famous Stalingrad Tractor Works depended, according to its chief engineer, Demyanovich,[8] on 283 medium-sized and small factories as contractors. They had to supply no less than 4,300 kinds of machine parts. Twenty million roubles' worth of tractors, piled up in the yards of the Works, could not be delivered because indispensable parts were lacking. The missing parts amounted in value to only 100,000 roubles, but the management did not have this small sum at its disposal because it could not sell products without the missing parts. Thus the sluggishness of small contractors resulted—according to their big customer—in interrupted production and turnover and in desperate attempts to get money and needed materials. 'During the first eight months of 1940, the Tractor Works spent 200,000 roubles on telegrams and 250,000 roubles on traveling expenses.' The same story was told half a year later of another giant plant, the Rostov Works for Agricultural Engineering, which, as Dvinsky, representative of the Rostov Party Committee, complained at the 18th Party Conference (February 1941), was inadequately supplied with machine parts and other funded materials.[9]

A quite comprehensive censure of the supply system was published in 1940 in the Gosplan periodical: [10]

The supply system of the industrial People's Commissariats does not meet tasks set by Party and government for industry. The structure of supply organs is faulty . . . They are unwieldy and

[8] A. Demyanovich, 'On Sanctions, Planning and the Responsibility of Managers,' *Pravda*, 27 October 1940.

[9] *Pravda*, 20 February 1941. See also, 'Limits of the Planning System,' in *Quarterly Bulletin of Soviet Russian Economics*, edited by S. N. Prokopovich (Geneva, December 1940), No. 6, *passim*, which cites many instances of cross-hauling and other defects of the supply system.

[10] A. Nesterovsky and R. Tzeitlin, 'Put Supply of Industry into Order!' in *Planned Economy* (1940), No. 3, pp. 50-59.

have numerous duplicating, superfluous links . . . The People's Commissariats have, for the most part, central procurement boards [*Glavsnabs*]. Each Glavsnab has one or several procurement trusts of Union-wide scale, and each supply trust has local offices. The Glavks, too, have supply divisions with a network of local branches. Industrial trusts and single plants, construction trusts and individual building projects, also have their own procurement organizations . . . This results in a waste of considerable national resources. Many thousands of people [11] are diverted from productive work, the turnover of goods is slowed down, and in many cases an artificial scarcity of certain goods results.

These writers conclude that thorough-going reform is urgently needed. Supply organization must be simplified, duplicating organs abolished. Plants must get as much elbowroom as is compatible with the general supply plan. Supply agencies must not only draw up supply plans but also execute them. Goods must not be moved from plants to warehouses of supply organs, still less from one supply organ to another. Such reforms would lead to large economies.

Neither the 3 June 1938 decree, nor similar orders and instructions issued for other products, nor frequent reorganizations of supply organs proved satisfactory. Specialized industrial People's Commissariats created in 1938-40 [12] imitated the old ones in building up supply organs.

At the outbreak of the war, Soviet economists and plant managers were still complaining about defects in the supply system. Radical reform in this field must have been one of the most urgent tasks of Soviet economy on the eve of the war.

[11] There are about 5,000 supply agencies subordinated to the supply organs of the 26 industrial Commissariats or their Glavks. More than 126,000 men are employed by them, with annual salary amounting to 518 million roubles. The cost of the services of supply constituted 11 per cent of their turnover value. See A. Nesterovsky and R. Tzeitlin, op. cit. p. 51.

[12] See Chapter I.

VI

Output, Cost, Profit, Price

a. Output and Measurement of Success

ONE of the plant manager's main tasks is to organize machinery to record quantitative, qualitative, and financial results of production. Results are compared currently with the tekhpromfinplan. A statistical department records quantitative results, the bookkeeping department, financial results.

1. *Quantity*. Reports on quantity of output and quantity of goods in process are compiled annually, quarterly, or monthly, on report forms prepared by central agencies for industrial statistics. The following 'indicators' are recorded: (1) volume of output and sales, in natural and monetary units; (2) volume and kind of capital investment; (3) number of workers and labor productivity; (4) working capital (stocks of finished products, materials, fuel; cash and bank deposits); (5) pay roll, by categories of workers; (6) detailed cost of production (for every operation and item produced); (7) expenses for fuel, electric power, raw materials, and semi-finished goods. Furthermore, the plant's statistical, planning, and bookkeeping departments measure and report in detail the degree of utilization of machines and equipment (percentage of optimum utilization), raw materials and fuel (consumption per unit of output), and labor (working hours per unit of goods produced, number of frames or benches per worker, ratio of auxiliary to direct labor, etc.).

The diversity of indicators in regular reports, as well as the great number of supervising instances demanding such reports, encumbers plant management. During 1939 the People's Commissariat for Heavy Machine Building called for reports on 176 forms with 235,000 indicators. Reports to the People's Commissariat for Chemicals required 172 forms, those to the People's Commissariat for Medium Machine Building, 180, etc. In 1940 the central government cut the number of reports by 40 to 55 per cent.[1] Even so, reports are still considered too numerous and complicated.

Volume of production is computed by plant statistical departments in 'roubles of 1926-7,' while bookkeeping departments record the monetary value of production. The measurement of production volume was established in 1926-7 when a schedule of products and current prices was set up. The quantity of each commodity produced is weighted by the price in 1926-7, and the sum of such weighted quantities gives the total volume of production independent of price fluctuations. The method has obvious defects, in that new goods were introduced after 1926-7, and that the price relations of that time (when industrial reconstruction had just begun after the ravages of the Civil War) are not typical of later years. The official schedule, on which the calculation is based, is revised from time to time by adding new products or by changing weightings. This compensates in part for shortcomings inherent in the very concept of a real volume of production. Since 1940, only gross output (i.e. production for internal plant use as well as for sale) has been calculated in 'real units.' Output for sale is quoted at current prices only. So is the value of goods in production. Special tables fix the relative value added at various stages of processing.[2]

During the first years of industrialization, many plant reports failed to give an adequate idea of work performed. The inclination was to estimate the success of a plant manager or a chief engineer by the amount of output. Accordingly, managers strove to increase quantity of production at the expense of quality.

[1] *Planned Economy* (1940), No. 11, p. 128.
[2] A. D. Mikhailov, *Industrial Statistics* (Moscow, 1939), pp. 20-22.

They leaned toward more easily produced qualities or poorly finished products. Reports lacked exactness and sometimes were simply fictitious.[3]

The government has carried on a fight against misrepresentation of facts in plant reports. Higher industrial agencies send inspectors to check production. Production plans submitted by plants are laid out in increasing detail, with fixed standards of production and norms of quality for every item.

2. *Quality*. In 1930 the chairman of the Supreme Council of National Economy, V. Kuibyshev, stated at a conference on the quality of production that 'in the struggle for quality we have thus far achieved nothing; worse than that, we must admit that we seem to be moving backward. We boast about a 100 per cent and a 150 per cent fulfilment of Plan, while at the same time we allow a considerable deterioration of quality.'[4]

Actually, the struggle for rapid increase in quantity hampered improvement of quality. The percentage of rejects in metal production was very high. Tractors were produced that could stand only a short period of wear. Mass consumption goods did not satisfy even the simplest taste. To raise the quality of production, certain criteria have been worked out. Plants must report the proportion of production definitely rejected or sent back for alterations; degree of deviation from standards; proportion of higher and lower grades; fulfilment of planned assortment, etc. In 1936 People's Commissar S. Ordzhonikidze ordered an investigation of the quality of production in heavy industry. It was declared that 'quality is becoming one of the cornerstones of our future development. High rejectage eats up huge sums of money.'[5] In 1939, another investigation of quality showed similar results. 'The cost of rejects and of defective goods in heavy in-

[3] R. Beshev, 'The Stakhanov Movement and Labor Productivity,' in *Problems of the Economy* (1936), No. 2, pp. 52-3. A. Zvorykin, 'Stakhanov Norms Compared Internationally,' in *Bolshevik* (1936), No. 17, pp. 43-50.

[4] *Pravda*, 10 October 1930.

[5] *For Industrialization*, 5 May 1936.

dustry has been estimated at several billion roubles annually.'[6] (Total production in that industry was estimated at somewhat more than 100 billion roubles.) Losses in machine building arising from high rejectage amounted on the average to 5.3 per cent of the cost of production, but this average was far exceeded by some plants (17.8 per cent at the Hammer and Sickle Works in Kharkov).[7] In metallurgy, sub-standard production amounted in the first half of 1940 to 6.5 per cent, and in some rolling-mills reached 15 per cent.[8] These figures included, it is true, products culled for refinishing. Even so, the figures must be considered high, in view of the fact that inspection standards, outside the defense industry, were relatively modest.

In a special decree of 10 July 1940, the Presidium of the Supreme Soviet prescribed five to eight years' imprisonment for managers, chief engineers, and plant heads of technical supervision convicted of incomplete, sub-standard, or defective production.[9] During the years immediately preceding the war, the tremendous efforts to raise the quality of industrial production, especially in the fields of metallurgy and machine building, greatly raised the economic potential of Soviet industry.

b. Cost

1. '*Business accountability.*' During the first years after the nationalization of industry (1918-20), years of civil war and tremendous inflation, plants were not required and did not attempt to maintain any relation between the amount of raw materials, fuel, and man power used and the quantity of goods produced. Plants received from State procurement agencies raw materials and fuel on a scanty scale; other State organs supplied workers with meager rations of food, clothing, and shelter. Plants were

[6] S. Turetski, 'Economics of Production and Quality Indicators,' in *Planned Economy* (1940), No. 8, p. 12.
[7] A. G. Zverev, *The State Budget for* 1940 (Moscow, 1940), p. 8.
[8] V. Petrovski, 'The Struggle for the Quality of Metal,' in *Planned Economy* (1940), No. 12.
[9] *Pravda*, 11 July 1940.

not held to account for the use of production factors, or compelled to compare costs with revenue.

Since the NEP, all industrial plants have worked on the principle of *khozraschet* (literally, business calculation or accountability), a term which, in Soviet law and economic literature, means measuring and maximizing efficiency of outlay.[10] Within the framework of the Plan and the limits set by available capital, plants now purchase and sell for money, at State-fixed prices. They must try to keep the cost of production below these prices.

This implies cost accounting. Unit costs of production must be calculated, and the excess of price over unit cost determined with some precision. Accordingly, books are kept in every industrial plant, and periodical balance-sheets are worked out in the usual way.

2. *The chief accountant.* The chief accountant is a leading management official. No payments are made without his signature. For a long time subordinated directly to the Trust or the Glavk which appointed him, he was the eye of the higher administration supervising the financial work of the plant manager. But as one-man control increased, such a division of power resulted in friction. After many legal changes, the chief accountant came to be appointed either by the manager or by the Trust (or Glavk) with his agreement. The chief accountant is subordinate to the manager and must carry out all his orders. Remnants of his former role remain, however.

The chief accountant, in line with the manager, is fully responsible for observing financial, budgetary and other estimates. He is also responsible for orderly bookkeeping and accounting . . . As far as the methods of bookkeeping are concerned, the

[10] The instruction 'On carrying out the principles of the new economic policy' (issued by the Council of People's Commissars on 9 August 1921) and the 'Basic regulations on the reconstruction of large size industry and on the increase and development of production' (issued by the Labor and Defense Council on 12 August 1921) are the earliest official documents in which the Soviet government formulated principles of profitability and business accountability.

chief accountant is directly subordinate to the bookkeeping department of the Trust or People's Commissariat.[11]

Only when a manager's order concerning finances is obviously illegal should the chief accountant, after having warned the manager, inform the Trust or the People's Commissariat of his refusal to carry out an order of the manager and give reasons therefor. This problem, however, is not definitely solved. As late as 1940, one of the chief accountants of the Kirov Works (Leningrad) wrote to *Pravda*:

> In practice there are often conflicts between the principle of one-man control, on the one hand, and the two, sometimes incompatible, functions of the chief accountant, on the other hand. The latter must be assistant to the manager in the field of finances; but at the same time he must supervise the financial transactions of the manager.[12]

Pravda, *Industry*, and *Machine Building* in 1939 and 1940 published much material on practical difficulties in co-operation between manager and chief accountant, the 'engineer of bookkeeping,' as he is called in the U.S.S.R.

3. *Planned and actual costs.* Almost simultaneously with the approval of the first Five Year Plan, the Central Committee of the Communist Party resolved, on 5 December 1929, that 'monthly plant statements be based on actual cost of production . . . The difference between planned and actual cost of production—provided quality requirements are absolutely satisfied—is a basic indicator of the success of plant work.'

Planned cost of production is calculated by higher agencies (People's Commissariat, Glavk) to guide economizing efforts of managers. It changes with the size and quality of plant equipment, availability of raw materials, etc. To reduce actual cost of production to or below planned level is one of the manager's most important tasks, its achievement an important indication of success.

[11] Decree of 29 September 1932.
[12] *Pravda*, 26 September 1940.

Both planned and actual costs of production of each product are calculated on standard forms, which take into account direct cost of production (cost of basic and auxiliary materials, wages, payments for social and cultural needs), sinking fund, other overhead charges, sales costs, and taxes. Thus components of the cost of production are, on the whole, the same as in other countries, with the notable exception of interest on capital, brokerage, and advertising.

4. *Cost reduction.* For reasons of broad economic policy, as well as from the narrower fiscal point of view, the Soviet State is extremely interested in cutting production costs. It aims at the most economical utilization of resources. At the same time, the treasury is a participant in industrial profits.[13] In every Five Year Plan, cost reduction has been regarded as one of the most important tasks of plant managers. 'It is necessary gradually to bring prices of industrial commodities nearer the price level of the leading capitalist countries,' declared the first Five Year Plan.[14] Its authors did not, of course, have in mind a comparison of money prices, which depend on foreign exchange rates. They meant a reduction of 'real' costs, especially of amounts of labor, raw materials, and equipment used per unit of production. The reduction percentages that follow were calculated by Soviet statisticians by assigning constant prices[15] to all cost elements except labor; labor was calculated at current money wage rates. Since, in all three Plan periods, an increase of money wage rates was both planned and achieved, planned and achieved cost-reduction figures would be larger than those shown below, if labor, too, were duly weighted with a constant rather than its current price.

The first Five Year Plan set as a goal an average of 35 per cent reduction of costs of industrial production; the reduction achieved was 12.3 per cent. The second Five Year Plan aimed at

[13] See c, below.

[14] Gosplan, *Five Year Plan for the Development of the National Economy of the U.S.S.R.* (Moscow, 1929), 1:107.

[15] Prices of 1926-7 in the first two Plans; of 1937 in the third Plan.

a reduction of 26 per cent; the achievement was 10.3 per cent.[16] The third Five Year Plan, in line with the experience of the preceding two, called for a reduction of 10 per cent.[17]

The following breakdown of aggregate cost reduction, as planned in a draft of the third Five Year Plan, gives an interesting picture of the tasks confronted. Reduction, expressed in per cent of total costs at the beginning of the period, had to be achieved by: (1) raising labor efficiency more rapidly than wage rates (3.8 per cent); (2) improving utilization of raw materials (4.4 per cent); (3) economizing on fuel and electric power (.6 per cent); (4) reducing administrative charges and overhead (1.4 per cent). The planned reduction of cost thus totaled 11.1 per cent. At the same time a .1 per cent increase in contributions to the sinking fund was planned so that the total planned reduction of costs was 11 per cent.[18] As finally approved in the Plan, the figure is 10 per cent.

Between 1925 and 1930, Soviet industry achieved an average reduction of 18.7 per cent in 'real' cost of production. During 1931-2, management and workers had obvious difficulties in adapting themselves to new and complicated plants built during the first Five Year Plan, and cost of production rose slightly. During the second Five Year Plan, however, it fell by 10.3 per cent on the average. In some branches the fall was much more (machine building, 45 per cent; heavy chemistry, 30 per cent; metallurgy, 20 per cent), in others less (foods, 7 to 8 per cent; timber and light industry, 3 to 5 per cent).[19]

To reduce industrial costs, the government applied various measures: 'flying inspection,' investigations, bonuses, fines. The

[16] Economic Institute of the Academy of Sciences, *Economics of Socialist Industry* (Moscow, 1940), pp. 502-17; S. Turetski, 'Socialist Accumulation,' in *Planned Economy* (1939), No. 3, p. 169.

[17] V. Molotov, *The Third Five Year Plan*, Address to the 18th Party Congress (Moscow, 1939), pp. 35-6.

[18] S. Turetski, op. cit. p. 169.

[19] S. Turetski, *The Cost of Production and the Problems of Price Structure* (Moscow, 1940), p. 120.

cost of production of a single commodity varies from plant to plant. Often this is owing not to objective causes but to failures of management, inadequate mastery of technique, or deficient workshop discipline. To reduce such failures, the government has frequently organized contests between individual workers, workshops, or whole plants. In 1939, for example, a big drive was launched to reduce production costs in metals, following an investigation which showed enormous cost differentials between plants. At the Kirovorgrad copper works the cost was higher than at the Krasnouralsk works, mainly because expenses per ton for auxiliary workers and workshop administration amounted at the former to 86 + 322 roubles, compared with 6 + 300 roubles at the latter.[20]

As is well known, labor efficiency before the First World War was much lower in Russia than in the leading industrial countries. For example, in tons per worker year, 1913 pig iron production in Russia, England, Germany, and the United States was, respectively, 205, 356, 400, 811.[21] During the first years of the Revolution, general economic disorganization and decline of workshop discipline further lowered labor efficiency; according to one estimate, the average annual output per worker in 1920 was about one-fourth of what it had been in 1913.[22]

During the period of industrialization (1928-40), economic leaders undertook many vigorous measures to raise labor efficiency, mainly by increasing workshop discipline and intensity of effort, but also by improving machinery and better utilizing raw materials and fuel. By the Second World War, labor efficiency had increased considerably. A Gosplan commission found that annual output per worker in 1928 was 4.557; 6.229 in 1932, and 11.386 roubles in 1937 (1926-7 prices).[23] The increase in labor efficiency continued during the third Five Year Plan, al-

[20] S. Turetski, op. cit. p. 120; *Economics of Socialist Industry*, p. 517.
[21] *Iron and Coal Trades Review* (London, 1922); *Stahl und Eisen* (1934).
[22] I. Kuz'minov, *The Stakhanovite Movement* (Moscow, 1940), pp. 183-4.
[23] Y. Joffe, *U.S.S.R. and the Capitalist Countries* (Moscow, 1939), p. 75.

though, in the words of a resolution proposed by Voznesenski, Chairman of Gosplan, 'in 1940 the possibilities of raising labor productivity were not utilized in full.' [24]

Reports on the fulfilment of the first Five Year Plan indicated an increase of 41 per cent in labor efficiency, as against a planned increase of 60 per cent. The second Five Year Plan brought about an increase of 82 as against a planned increase of 63 per cent. Reports on the first three years of the third Five Year Plan indicate an increase of 38 as against a planned increase of 65 per cent for the entire five-year period.[25]

These average data for all industry are based on constant weights (prices of 1926-7) assigned to the various products. They are confirmed by more precise and reliable figures of per capita physical output of individual industries. These figures indicate that the difference between Soviet labor efficiency and that of England and Germany is diminishing, although Soviet is still very far from American efficiency. While national differences in definitions make exact international comparison impossible, the general trend can hardly be doubted.[26]

No errors involved in the computation of Soviet figures can

[24] 'Resolution on the Report of Voznesenski to the Conference of the Communist Party, February 1941,' in *Bolshevik* (1941), No. 3-4, p. 66.

[25] E. Vasil'ev and Kh. Koval'son, 'Increase of Labor Efficiency,' in *Planned Economy* (1939), No. 3; S. Kheinman, 'On Reserves of Man Power and Labor Efficiency,' in *Problems of the Economy* (1940), No. 11-12, p. 106.

[26] The annual output of coal in tons per basic worker in 1929 and 1937 was respectively 179 and 370 in the U.S.S.R.; 323 and 435 in Germany; 844 and 730 in the United States. The annual output of pig iron per blast-furnace worker was in Russia, 1929: 240 tons; 1937: 756 tons; in England, 1932: 366 tons; 1937: 513 tons; in the United States, 1929: 1,729 tons; 1937: 1,620 tons. The annual output per worker in the cotton textile industry was, in Russia, 1929: 4,938 sq. meters; 1937: 8,200 sq. meters; in the United States, 1929: 16,800 sq. meters; 1937: 17,650 sq. meters. See Joffe, op. cit. p. 78; League of Nations, *World Production and Prices*, 1938-9 (Geneva, 1940), and *Statistical Yearbook of the League of Nations*, 1940-41 (Geneva, 1942); *Statistical Abstract of the United States*, 1941 (Washington, 1942). For a critical appraisal, see A. Yugow, *Russia's Economic Front for War and Peace: An Appraisal of the Three Five Year Plans* (New York, 1942), pp. 179, 186-7.

be so great as to justify doubts in regard to the main facts: technical reconstruction and strengthened workshop discipline have raised labor efficiency, chiefly through more intensive labor. There are still poor arrangement of tools and insufficient or uneven mechanization. But on the whole, machines and benches are better utilized than before; breakage and idling of machines have diminished; speed has increased. The outlay of fuel, electric power, and metal has approached planned norms, despite delays in the supply of fuel and materials, and red tape in management. The number of auxiliary workers has decreased, although it is in many cases still five to eight times larger than in similar American plants. The raised performance norms for pieceworkers [27] and such means of encouraging efficient labor as 'shock work,' the Stakhanovite movement, etc., carried through during the years 1936, 1938, and 1939, played a major part in the improvement.[28]

In the struggle for greater efficiency, the plant manager and his technical staff play an important and responsible part. Some measures designed to increase labor intensity and establish order, including decrees of the central government requiring increase of performance norms and improvement of quality and declaring a war on 'shirkers,' have not been popular with workers. In carrying out these measures, managers have often met sharp dissatisfaction. At least as difficult were, on the other hand, the tasks arising in connection with the Stakhanovite movement: managers and technical staff ran into the complicated problem of putting a brake on the excesses of this movement while supporting its valuable elements.

In his speech to the First All-Union Conference of Stakhanovites (17 November 1935) Stalin pointed out that 'to a certain degree, the Stakhanovite movement was conceived and began to develop against the will of plant management, even in a struggle

[27] See Chapter III.C.

[28] V. Molotov, *The Third Five Year Plan* (Moscow, 1939), p. 37; S. Kheinman, op. cit.; reports of Malenkov and Voznesenski at the 18th Party Conference (February 1941); A. Yugow, op. cit. Chapter VIII.

with it. Management, at that time, did not help the Stakhanovite movement but opposed it.' [29] In fact, managers feared that Stakhanovites would infringe on the entire order of plant work and break rules imposed by the technological process. Stakhanovites often overfulfilled production assignments at the expense of lasting disorganization of the work rhythm. They undermined departmental subordination as well as the authority of the technical staff and of the manager himself. Nevertheless, the leaders of Soviet economy demanded that the manager not only direct and help the Stakhanovite movement, but initiate and inspire it. 'The increase of labor efficiency depends on commanders of production,' wrote *Pravda* (29 April 1938). For many managers and engineers, such intricate maneuvering between government, Stakhanovites, and workers was too much. During the period of the Stakhanovite movement, many managers had to give way to those better fitted for this particular task. This was one aspect of the 'purges' of 1936-8, whose political causes we cannot treat here.[30]

5. *Overhead and sinking funds.* Overhead charges have decreased. Soviet economists make much of the fact that overhead charges represent no more than 6 per cent of cost and are considerably lower than in other countries. They regard this circumstance as an advantage of State-planned economy. Nationalization of production and distribution resulted, of course, in a decrease of advertising expenses. Moreover, no interest on capital or insurance is included in costs. On the other hand, red tape, administrative confusion, and lack of commercial skill have been obstacles to the reduction of costs. If, nevertheless, overhead and administrative charges debited to the cost of production in the books of individual plants are relatively small, this is because of accounting methods and does not represent the real role of administrative expenses in the national economy. For an essential part of the expenses of the administrative machine of industry (the organization of distribution, credit, transport, and storage)

[29] *Speech to the Conference of Stakhanovites* (Moscow, 1935), pp. 13-14.
[30] See also Chapter IX.

does not appear in plant budgets but in the State budget.[31] All these are, in fact, financed mainly out of the proceeds of the turnover tax.[32]

The change in attitude toward sinking funds is worthy of notice. In the beginning, the conviction prevailed that the creation of sinking funds for wear and tear of machines, buildings, transport equipment, etc., would be superfluous, since the State, not the individual plant, must replace means of production in State-owned industry. In fact, however, the State did not repair or replace industrial equipment. Plants and machines deteriorated.

Only after plants adopted business accountability did they begin to make contributions to a special sinking fund. Today the annual contribution to the sinking fund in leading industries (heavy, light, foods, etc.) is from 5.5 to 5.6 per cent of initial value of machines, equipment, and building.[33] Since 1938, 40 to 65 per cent (depending on the industry) of such contributions are at the disposal of the manager, while the rest is transmitted to central organs. In theory, that part of the sinking fund which is at the manager's disposal is merely for repairs. But, as a matter of fact, it is used for replacement as well. The part turned over to central organs is, in theory, to be used for replacements within the given industry. In practice, however, transfers in favor of other (especially heavy) industries have often taken place.[34]

c. Profits

The sales price of industrial goods is a sum of three components: (1) planned cost of production, (2) planned profit, and (3) turnover tax. All three, and hence price, are determined in advance by the government. But actual cost can be reduced below planned cost by efforts and ability of both management and

[31] On the size and functioning of the machinery distributing producers' goods, see Chapter v.c.

[32] See d, below.

[33] N. A. Blatov, *Principles of Industrial Accounting and Calculation* (Moscow, 1939), p. 127.

[34] Decree of 8 January 1938.

employees. This is the only way in which they can make actual profits exceed planned profits. The government, for instance, fixes the factory price for some item at 20 roubles, viz., 14 roubles production costs, 2 roubles planned profit, and 4 roubles (20 per cent) turnover tax. If plant management reduces the cost from 14 to, say, 10 roubles, the profit becomes 6 roubles, of which 2 are planned and 4 'above Plan.'

A plant's total profit is divided quarterly between it and higher organs of the industry, whose budgets form a part of the State budget. The ratio is fixed from time to time according to the needs of the industry, but in no case is the government share lower than 10 per cent. In 1937 all industry transmitted more than 48 per cent of its total profits to the State budget.[35] Of all federal revenues, contributions from industrial profits constituted 6 per cent in 1937, 12 per cent in 1940. As a rule, such contributions are used by government to finance industrial expansion, although subsidies for new industrial construction may be provided from other budgetary sources (mainly the turnover tax).

That part of plant profits which remains at the disposal of management is again divided between capital funds (to provide for expansion of fixed or working capital) and the so-called 'manager's fund.' Allocations to capital funds for expansion are thus independent from and in addition to a plant's allowances for sinking fund, which are for repairs only (or, in practice, repairs and replacement).

Until 1936 there existed in plants various funds for employees' bonuses and for the improvement of their conditions. In 1936 a unified fund at the disposal of the plant manager was created.[36] The 'manager's fund' is financed out of profits; 4 per cent of the planned profit and 50 per cent of profit 'above Plan' are allocated to it quarterly. Not less than one-half of the fund is to be used for housing workers and other employees, the remainder for

[35] *Economics of Socialist Industry* (cited above), p. 548.

[36] Decree of 19 April 1936; instruction of the Council of People's Commissars, 31 December 1936.

other services (crèches, kindergartens, clubs, canteens, etc.), for bonuses for outstanding work, and for rationalization and technical propaganda. Construction financed by the fund is independent of Plan provisions, although it requires Commissariat approval. Bonuses to individual workers are determined by the manager, after the aggregate shares of various groups (manual workers, clerical workers, Stakhanovites, etc.) are agreed on by him and the plant committee. Committee consent is also needed for other expenditures from this fund. The manager's special fund serves, nevertheless, to increase his power, prestige, and responsibility.

If higher local or central authorities find a plant unprofitable because of bad organization and incompetent management, they assume the responsibility of reorganizing it and removing disqualified personnel.[37] If the plant proves unprofitable as a result of an unexpected rise in the price of elements of production, the authorities revise the factory price of the product and the 'planned' cost of production. By the time of the outbreak of war, factory prices of industrial products had gradually been fixed at levels that secured profits to the overwhelming majority of industrial plants. Only a few, highly important for the Soviet State, continue to require subsidies to cover losses.

The above-mentioned regulations concerning profits have been in force since 31 December 1936. Formerly plants had to transmit all profits to higher organs, receiving grants under the State budget without reference to profitability. Thus profitable plants supported poorly managed and unprofitable plants.

In the first years after nationalization of industry, State-owned plants produced without profit and depended on State subsidies. This was not the effect of deliberate policy but the consequence of exhaustion and disorganization resulting from war, revolution, and rapid liquidation of private property. True, some Soviet economists then thought that State plants, unlike private ones,

[37] See Chapter VIII.

need not realize profit; they argued that organs of the socialist community must maintain and expand production not for profit but to satisfy consumer needs. The real economic problem of those days, however, was not to choose among methods of expanding production. Economic collapse resulted in what was called mass 'squandering': inventories were depleted and equipment deteriorated. With the beginning of the NEP, the situation improved. The 12th Congress of the Communist Party (1923) resolved that 'a country's industry can be victorious only if it yields more than it absorbs.'[38] The principles set forth in the regulations of 1921 were confirmed: it was decided that all plants should work on lines of 'business accountability,' operate without loss, and achieve a profit. As the entire Soviet economy grew stronger and, in particular, as the administration won proficiency in new methods, ever more industrial plants adopted business accountability.

In the case of consumers' goods, this could be achieved without delay. The buying public's money began to finance and bring profits to plants producing much desired and scarce articles of mass consumption. It was different, however, with producers' goods, where, unless the prices of the goods were raised, profits could emerge only after a delay. Machines, iron and steel, ores, coal, etc., were supplied, in the main, not to the public but to other State-owned plants, and the public's money was, at the beginning, accessible not through the market but through the State budget. The State had to subsidize producers' goods plants not only to ensure expansion, but also to cover running expenses; it took considerable time before sales of consumers' goods began to cover a more substantial part, although still not all, of the working expenses of heavy industries.

As late as 1936, wholesale prices for coal, metal, machines, tools, etc., were still below the cost of production and could yield no profits. For this policy the following reasons were offered:

[38] *Decisions*, 1:569.

Low prices for coal, metal, tools and machines create additional incentives in order that machine techniques shall take root in all branches of national economy. But if at the same time cost of production is high, the maintenance of relatively low prices for goods produced by heavy industry is possible only through State subsidies.[39]

Only when technical reconstruction had been largely completed and productivity increased, while the demand of agricultural collectives became stronger, could the State bring prices for coal, metal, and machines into relation to production costs, and require profits from heavy-industry plants.[40]

In the words of a Soviet economist, 'State subsidies created an attitude of dependence and irresponsibility on the part of some Soviet industrial managers, thus weakening the effects of business accountability.'[41] They also created a complete neglect of plant finances: 'Why worry? The subsidy will always cover losses!'[42]

Under the regime of accountability and profitability, subsidies have gradually become confined, on the whole, to the financing of new construction and of certain plants of particular State importance. The desire to increase profits has become a real incentive to more responsible, active, and careful management.

d. Indirect Taxation as the Main Price Factor

The manager is not only responsible for profit as a measure of the plant's success as a productive unit; he is also responsible for State revenue collected at the plant.

Until 1929, State-owned plants paid sixty-eight different taxes: trade and local indirect taxes, excise and various other duties. Numerous Soviet economists of that period recommended consolidating all contributions out of profits into a single tax on plants. The Central Committee of the Party decided to 'entrust

[39] M. Bogolepov, 'On Sales Prices in Industry,' in *Planned Economy* (1936), No. 5, pp. 76-7.

[40] Decree of 2 March 1936.

[41] M. Bogolepov, op. cit. pp. 76-7.

[42] *The Plan* (1936), No. 9, p. 8.

the People's Commissariat for Finances and the Supreme Council of National Economy with the elaboration of a tax system for State-owned plants on the basis of a single contribution out of profits.' As, however, many State-owned plants were then unprofitable, revenue was, for the time being, made dependent only to a limited extent on contributions from profits; it was supplemented by what became and still is the foundation of the entire taxation system: the turnover tax (sales tax).[43]

This was also the government's answer to another much discussed question: shall the tremendous and rapid 'super-industrialization' be financed by direct or indirect tax? The Soviet leaders chose the second road and transformed every plant into a tax-collecting instrument, giving the following reasons:

> The exchequer has in the turnover tax a resource not immediately dependent on the success or profitableness of an individual plant. This tax operates rather directly as an instrument of accumulating means for the State budget . . . Funds accumulated at the plant as tax revenue are distributed among the various plants and branches of industry according to Plan in order to expand production . . . The inclusion of the tax in the price of the item produced is not dictated by the direct needs of the individual plant.[44]

Every manager, then, must secure a high return of the turnover tax in addition to the contribution out of profits. The State fixes both the price and the turnover tax and receives the tax whether the plant is profitable or not. Small quantity or poor quality means not only that the manager has failed to fulfil Plan: he has also caused a loss of State revenue. Thus, turnover-tax requirements induce him to raise and improve output. At the same time, the State's claim to a share in profits makes it his official duty to strive for a reduction of cost.[45]

Price 'does not represent the money equivalent of the cost of

[43] Decision of 5 December 1929.

[44] V. D'yachenko, ed., *The Finances of the U.S.S.R.* (Moscow, 1935), pp. 19-21.

[45] See a, above.

production. It is the main instrument for the redistribution of the national income,' point out the heads of the Economic Institute of the Academy of Sciences.[46] Accordingly, reduction of cost does not ultimately result, as under free competition, in reduction of price. In an even more absolute way than the monopolistic corporations of the capitalist countries, the Soviet State may keep prices unchanged despite reduction of cost: State monopoly is complete. Reduction of cost may, therefore, wholly or in part, result in increased plant profits and State revenue, instead of in lowered prices. So far, cost economies have been used in the main for general needs of the national economy or defense and, in the case of profitable plants, to improve working and living conditions of employees (via the manager's fund). Not more than one-third to one-half of all cost economies achieved during the three Plan periods can have been used for reductions in sales prices.[47]

The turnover tax (more than 2,500 individual rates) is imposed on almost all consumption goods at the point where they leave the producing plant and enter channels of distribution. Rates (in per cent of retail price) vary greatly: grain and bread, 75 per cent; cattle and meat, 62 to 70 per cent; butter, 50 to 66 per cent; salt, 82 per cent; vegetables, 30 per cent; tea, coffee, 86 per cent; pastries and cakes, 56 per cent; tobacco, 80 per cent; alcohol, 90 per cent; textile fabrics, 74 per cent; shoes 70 to 86 per cent; rubbers, 60 per cent; soap, 62 per cent; petroleum, 67 per cent; matches, 70 per cent; exercise books, 10 to 25 per cent; etc.[48] For example, the retail price of sugar in 1940 was fixed at 6.50 roubles per kilogram, of which 5.20 roubles represented turnover tax.

Thus, retail prices are completely divorced from costs. The

[46] *Economics of Socialist Industry* (cited above), p. 498.

[47] Gosplan, *Five Year Plan for the Development of the National Economy of the U.S.S.R.* (Moscow, 1929), I:85, 107, and *The Second Five Year Plan* (Moscow, 1934), II:367. For the third Five Year Plan, see S. Turetski, 'Socialist Accumulation,' in *Planned Economy* (1939), No. 3, pp. 168-9.

[48] *Bulletin for Economic and Financial Law* (1934 and 1935); P. Yabukhtin, *Taxes under Capitalism and in the Soviet Economy* (Moscow, 1935), pp. 59-60, 68; *Laws and Ordinances*, 1939-40.

selection of the object of taxation, the level of the tax rates, their automatic nature which provides for no exempted minimum or payment in installments, impart to this tax all the objectionable features of indirect taxation.[49]

On the other hand, this tax has proved very expedient as a source of revenue, easy to collect and difficult to evade because, under State monopoly, the citizen cannot get a pound of bread, a yard of cloth, or a pound of coal unobserved by the government.

The turnover tax has provided the means for industrialization and defense on an immense scale in a short time, despite great obstacles. In recent years, more than 70 per cent of budget revenues were collected from the turnover of commodities or from profits of State-owned plants. In 1940, for example, 59.4 per cent of all revenue came from the turnover tax on industrial and agricultural products (105.8 billion roubles), while contributions out of the profits of industrial and other plants yielded another 12.3 per cent (more than 21 billion roubles). Direct and indirect taxes raised through other methods yielded only 5.3 per cent of revenues.[50]

The revenue from turnover tax differs from contributions from profits in that it must be paid by unprofitable as well as profitable plants. But since Soviet Russian industrial profits depend on State-fixed prices, the difference is illusory. The turnover tax and contributions from profits may both be regarded as indirect taxes, or both may be considered contributions by industry to State revenue.

Proceeds from turnover tax and profit contributions cannot be compared with the tax receipts of other countries, unless one bears in mind that the budget of the Soviet government contains not only revenues *from* industry (in both forms) but also con-

[49] For details see A. Yugow, op. cit. p. 132.

[50] A. G. Zverev, *Pravda*, 26 February 1941. Further important items of the budget were: loans, 6.2 per cent; social-security contribution of plants, 5 per cent.

tributions *to* industry. Industry contributed to the State budget only 1.8 billion roubles more than it received from the State in the period of the first Five Year Plan. In the second Five Year period the difference was 85.1 billion roubles. During the third Five Year period, the total contribution of industry also exceeded its receipts from the State. As already mentioned, these receipts (especially in more recent times) go to support new industrial construction: capital investments were financed by the State to the amount of 24.8 billion roubles in the first Five Year period, 65.8 billion roubles in the second.[51]

[51] *Economics of Socialist Industry* (cited above), pp. 530-31.

VII

'Control by the Rouble'

AS industrial plants went over to business accountability, and State subsidies gradually became rarer, bank credit had to be restored. State and co-operative banks emerged under the NEP (1921-8), operating on rules common throughout the world: they were supposed to grant short- and long-term credit to solvent plants, accept commodities as collateral, discount bills, cash checks, etc. The banking system differed from that of other countries in two important respects: the question of interest was unsettled, and depositors were State plants and agencies (including co-operatives) rather than consumers.[1] The latter could deposit savings in special savings institutions only; deposits by small private businessmen reappeared during the NEP but were discontinued after a few years.

The peculiar character of Soviet bank clients naturally affected banking functions. As industrialization was speeded, State banks often felt impelled, occasionally by government influence, to grant credit without considering commercial rules of profitableness and liquidity. Often, as a matter of fact, long- and short-term credits became outright grants. For if a State-owned plant failed to honor a promissory note, it was obviously out of the question to sell it at auction. Much friction arose between banks and managers, who rather frequently indulged in 'kite-flying' (accommodation bills), borrowing money without underlying commodity transactions.

[1] M. Sobolev, *The Main Problems of Credit Organization* (Moscow, 1929), p. 11.

By a decree of 30 January 1930, the Council of People's Commissars tried to reform the credit system. According to this decree, credits could be granted only in accordance with the approved plant tekhpromfinplan and only in line with progress in its realization.[2] This meant the end of ordinary commercial credits and bill discounts. It meant, in effect, control of industry by banks. This reform was applied suddenly and led to financial chaos in plants.

Banks first showed themselves unable to cope with their new duties: they could not check plans of all industrial managers, except perfunctorily. At best, they checked on the existence of this or that item in a plan. Whenever banks attempted to use their full authority, industrial agencies complained of 'bank dictatorship.' Two quotations will illustrate the disorganization and struggle. The State Bank point of view:

Men who have lost the habit of real management and prefer to live at the expense of the State Bank are unable to conceive that the property of a bankrupt can be put up for sale at auction.[3]

The point of view of industrial officials:

Is it possible that the State Bank is going to distrain on Magnitostroi for overspending the planned allowance? And to just whom will the State Bank contrive to sell a State railroad operating at a deficit? [4]

Two years after the decree was issued, the head of the People's Commissariat for Finances, Grinko, stated that 'the credit reform of 1930 led to consequences directly opposite to its aims and inflicted considerable damage upon our national economy.' [5] The reform had abolished the old principles of commercial guarantees and collateral, without giving precise and practicable form to the new principle of 'crediting on plan.'

[2] See Chapter IV.d and Chapter VI.a.1.
[3] *For Industrialization*, 21 April 1931.
[4] *Pravda*, 10 May 1931.
[5] *Finances and Socialist Economy* (1931), No. 12, p. 17.

After little more than a year, the central administration found itself compelled to amend the sudden and oversimplified credit reform of 1930. Decrees issued in the first part of 1931 [6] considerably altered relations between banks and industry. In addition, plants received outright allotments of working capital (a measure omitted from the old decree with dire consequences) in accordance with production programs and needs. This made them less urgently dependent on bank credit.

Long-term credits are now granted, in accordance with directions of planning organs, by specialized government banks (one for industry, another for agriculture and co-operatives).

For short-term credits, an attempt has been made to combine 'crediting on plan' with commercial principles. Short-term credits are granted by the State Bank for specific expenditures, which must conform to a plant's approved plan, or to supply agreements [7] between plants. The Bank must also consider the solvency of the plant applying for credit.

Thus, the banks do, in effect, perform a task of financial inspection for the government. They also have the right to supervise the efficiency of office organization, methods of bookkeeping and cost accounting, commercial operations, etc. But they may not interfere with technology of production or construction, or enforce payment transactions without the payer's consent, even if such payments are implied in the plan. Nor have they much to say concerning the merits of agreements and plans approved by higher instances.

These controlling functions of banks—summarily described in Soviet literature as 'control by the rouble'—are strengthened by a virtual suppression of inter-plant credits or cash-payments: all financial transactions of industry are carried on through banks (State Bank for short-term credits and Industrial Bank for long-term credits). No bills can be accepted in payment between plants. Instead, direct money orders of planning agencies have

[6] 1 January, 1 February, 20 March, 23 July.
[7] See Chapter v.

come into use. More important are checks drawn by managers: all plants are compelled to keep deposits with the State Bank. The State Bank transfers money from one current account to another only on order of the depositor and in accordance with approved plans.[8] State-owned plants may not hold funds in cash nor are they, as a rule, allowed to settle financial relations with each other on a cash basis. No manager may pay cash except for wages and salaries; these payments, however, are subject to bank supervision, except for payments under 1,000 roubles.[9]

The present credit system ostensibly applies methods created by capitalist society, but the differences are substantial. It is true that in other countries, too, banks have, in varying degree, insight into or even control over industrial production. They supervise, to some extent, planning of debtor corporations and may develop economic policy. In the U.S.S.R., however, these functions are normal banking duties. Since, furthermore, all economic activities are under strict State control, with the State virtual proprietor of all means of production, bank control is merely a form of State control.

After the first loud protest against 'control by the rouble,' relations between banks and industrial organs gradually became more normal, particularly after some working capital was granted to plants and banking functions were more cautiously defined. The new system has made possible plant financial operations on what seems to be a tolerably clear and uniform basis.

[8] N. A. Blatov, *Principles of Industrial Accounting and Calculation* (Moscow, 1939), pp. 20-21.

[9] Decrees of 14 January 1931 (Art. 13), and 15 August 1939.

VIII

Incentives

a. Advancement and Remuneration

WE have seen under what close supervision the plant manager and his whole leading staff work. Systematic reports are made regularly to higher agencies. In addition, work is under the close observation of representatives of the State Bank, local Party committees, and, to some extent, trade unions. Reports must be made to workers' production conferences. The activity of the manager and his assistants is thus constantly stimulated or interfered with by numerous organs. The general and specialized press constantly discuss conditions in individual plants. Moreover, nearly every plant has a 'wall newspaper' (run by the Party organization in the plant or, less frequently, by the workers' plant committee), to record achievements and castigate mismanagement.

The manager is appointed by the State agency to which the plant is subordinated (e.g. Commissariat, Glavk, Trust). Working-class origin, Party membership, and the patronage of influential dignitaries were long decisive in the appointment of industrial leaders. Only since about 1935 has 'bourgeois' descent lost importance as an obstacle to nomination to a leading position. The part played by patronage has also become somewhat less pronounced. But Party membership has retained decisive importance. The higher a managerial position, the more likely is its holder to be a Party member.[1] Preference has, however, also been given to contributors to pre-term fulfilment of Plan, reduction of

[1] See b, below.

production costs, or improvement of quality. Particularly efficient and talented workers (e.g. many Stakhanovites) have been sent to technical schools and later appointed managers of plants or Trusts. Instances of advancement for quality of work and energy are numerous.[2] On the other hand, there are numerous instances of dismissal and rebuke of managers and assistants for non-fulfilment of Plan, 'connivance with idlers,' etc.[3]

It would seem that two of the main incentives to energetic management are advancement for successes, and demotion or punishment for deficiencies—a system reminiscent of civil-service rules and customs in other countries or, better, of an army.

The manager and leading staff receive both monetary compensation and compensation in kind, chiefly in the form of apartments, free transportation, etc. Furthermore, their work is stimulated by bonuses in money or kind. In fact, the regular money salary is often of less importance than are bonuses.

During the first years of the Revolution, leading personnel received remuneration according to a comprehensive schedule, embracing all employees down to manual workers, and fixing relative wage rates. The schedule of 1921, which remained valid for some years, set the following relative rates or 'coefficients' (using the lowest rate as a unit): manual and lower clerical workers 1 to 2.7; other clerical workers 1.2 to 3.5; technical personnel 1.6 to 5.0; leading administrative personnel, 4.0 to 5.0.[4] Thus changes in

[2] Specialized industrial periodicals such as *Industry*, *Machine-Building*, *Steel*, *Light Industry*, and others, often publish biographies of managers, describing advancement due to energy and initiative.

[3] 'For non-fulfilment of Plan,' managers of Traktorodetal, Karbyurator, Russki Diesel, Glavarambit, were dismissed. The managers of the Economiser, Mytishchenski, and Stankozavod plants were brought to trial 'for not complying with orders on strengthening discipline.' Eight managers were removed and six others reproved by the People's Commissariat of the Defense Industry 'for connivance with shirking.' The manager and leading staff of the Voroshilovgrad Works were tried 'for preposterous inefficiency.' See *Industry*, 28 December 1938; *Machine-Building*, 3 and 27 January, 2 February, 2 July, 3 August 1939.

[4] Instruction of the Central Trade Union Council of 1 December 1921. For details see S. Schwarz, *Der Arbeitslohn und die Lohnpolitik in Russland* (Jena, 1924), pp. 46-9.

staff remuneration automatically followed changes in lower wage categories.

In the mid- and late twenties this tie was gradually broken, and separate schedules were established for technical and managerial staffs. In 1929 a schedule of absolute salary rates was fixed for officials of higher industrial agencies, and in 1933 for leading staffs of industrial plants, analogous to civil-service salary lists in other countries.[5] This general schedule has been revised from time to time since 1938 by the Economsoviet.[6]

The classification of each employee is fixed by the appointing body. In many cases, however, general rates are superseded by 'personal' rates, usually fixed by the People's Commissar. As a rule, these must not exceed 150 per cent of the general rates. Personal rates may exceed 2,000 roubles per month (1,400 in certain small industries) only with the special permission of the Council of People's Commissars.[7]

Data on managers' salaries are scanty. Some inferences may be drawn from salaries of their highest subordinates, chief engineers. In the Donbas coal mines, these received in 1933, depending on the type of mine, from 550 to 1,100 roubles per month. In larger mines, salaries could be further raised, by agreement between manager and Trust, to 1,500 roubles per month.[8] In iron and steel, regular engineers' salaries in 1939 were 600 to 1,500 roubles per month.[9] The overall monthly average for technical personnel (engineers, technicians, foremen) in the third quarter of 1940 was 1,223 roubles in the Sickle and Hammer open hearths in Moscow,[10] 1,570 roubles in a coal mine near by (Bolokhovugol').[11]

[5] *Laws and Ordinances*, 1929:737; 1933:75.

[6] Ibid. 1938:178.

[7] Ibid. 1938:229. Recent changes, if any, are unknown to the authors.

[8] Ibid. 1933:183. In that year the monthly average earnings of coal-mining manual workers was 132.60 roubles; see Central Statistical Office, *Socialist Construction in the U.S.S.R.* (Moscow, 1936), p. 524.

[9] Order of the Commissariat for Ferrous Metallurgy of 16 July 1939, in *Industry*, 21 July 1939.

[10] *Pravda*, 24 October 1940. At the same plant, average earnings of workers at the open hearth were 604 roubles.

[11] *Pravda*, 29 October 1940.

As a result of the chronic shortage of experienced technicians and other specialists, many often held two positions, e.g. chief engineer in a plant and paid lecturer in a technical school or expert for a planning organ. Although in 1933 a government decree [12] sought to abolish 'plurality of jobs,' special authorizations were easily obtainable and considerable plurality continued. More recently, the shortage of engineers has been partly overcome, and overspecialized technical teaching has been somewhat reduced; plurality of jobs has consequently become rarer.

As a rule, a successful manager or chief engineer enjoys personal use of a car and chauffeur; free family vacations in a rest home, including transportation; or perhaps a factory apartment or cottage–of special value in a country with acute housing shortage. Not only the material welfare, but also the social standing of the manager depend, in fact, on remuneration in kind. Of two managers or engineers receiving equal salaries and bonuses, the one who lives in a large cottage with a garden and car is far better off than his colleague who occupies a cramped apartment and rides in the streetcar. In the newspaper of heavy industry, engineer E. Strekalov declared:

> I am living in clover, I earn much money. I have more than 16,000 roubles in bonuses. Last summer I was with my wife and son at a health resort. I have bought a complete set of furniture for my apartment. One thing is lacking: my apartment is not good.[13]

The bonuses which managers, chief engineers, and section heads receive depend on the extent of overfulfilment of Plan, as measured by output, cost of production, and other indicators.[14] Bonuses in heavy industry are illustrative. In coal mining, for each per cent of reduction of real cost of production below planned cost, the manager, assistant manager, chief and assistant engineers get a bonus of 15 per cent of monthly salary. In iron and steel industry, the figure is 10 per cent.

[12] Decree of 11 March 1933.

[13] *Industry*, 31 December 1937.

[14] For details see Chapter VI.

Furthermore, for each per cent of overfulfilment of planned output, the bonus for a coal-mine manager and his immediate assistants is 4 per cent of salary.[15] In iron and steel, bonuses for extra output are calculated progressively. If pig-iron production exceeds Plan by 5 per cent, the monthly salaries of a section head, assistant section head, engineer, and electrical engineer are raised 10 per cent for each per cent of excess output. If the production excess is 10 per cent, the bonus for each per cent of excess output is 15 per cent of monthly salary, etc.

Occasionally total annual bonuses granted manager or engineer equal or even surpass annual salary. One engineer received as bonuses for pre-term completion of two boring machines, 8,320 and 8,000 roubles; [16] a manager received 12,000 roubles in bonuses for pre-term fulfilment of Plan and lowering of production costs.[17] During recent years particularly large bonuses have been introduced for outstanding inventions and improvements in technique or organization. In April 1942, several so-called 'Stalin bonuses' were granted leading staffs of industrial plants, in some cases amounting to 50, 100, and 150 thousand roubles.[18]

Since plant profits [19] are increased by lowered cost or increased production, bonuses for cost reduction or overfulfilment are related to profits, although not as a rule calculated as a percentage of profits. No less important is the effect of plant profits on managerial influence, prestige, and power. That part of profits remaining at the disposal of the manager is divided between capital fund and a special manager's fund for bonuses and improvement of workers' living conditions. Both uses increase managers' scope of action.

b. Intangibles

It may be that in Soviet Russia prestige and honor are more important and effective rewards and incentives than raises in in-

[15] Orders of the Commissariats for Fuel (20 June 1939) and for Ferrous Metallurgy (16 July 1939), *Industry*, 21 June and 21 July 1939, respectively.

[16] *Industry*, 31 December 1937.

[17] *Enterprise*, 29 August 1939.

[18] *Pravda*, 11 April 1942.

[19] See Chapter vi.c.

come, whether in money or in kind. One need not look at Russia to see promotion valued not only because of increased material enjoyments. And, of course, in a country affording little scope to luxury consumption and remunerative investment of savings, 'intangible' rewards can play a relatively great role. Still more interesting, perhaps, is the importance assigned in Soviet life to intangible and non-personal values. Consciousness of serving the country or the cause—'the socialist country'—influences many. Concrete cases of anonymous self-sacrifice are, by their nature, not easy to discover. Ordinarily the distinction between striving for careers and honor and working for a cause, between 'individualistic' and 'collectivistic' ('patriotic') motives, is not easily drawn.

Analysis is not made easier by the fact that existing material is, in the main, provided by an official press and in officially supervised literature. The student must be wary of slogans and official sentimentality. On the other hand, the very fact of ideological monopoly over a period of twenty years or more makes it probable that many people act or tend to act as represented in the articles and novels and other literature on which they have been brought up.

It is useful to strive to glimpse the 'spirit' of Soviet 'economic man,' to sense the psychological 'climate' surrounding and underlying economic activity in the U.S.S.R. It is not easy to separate the psychology of managerial personnel from that of others in industry. It may be assumed, however, that the frame of mind prevailing in the more active or better-paid strata of working masses is not much different from that of managers.

Photographs of managers, engineers, and workers distinguished through energy and success appear in local and central press organs and make men widely known. Those outstanding are decorated with the Emblem of Honor, the Order of the Red Labor Banner, or the Order of Lenin. Plant managers who have achieved pre-term fulfilment of Plan are mentioned in special honorary lists.[20]

The leaders of Soviet economy skillfully create the psychological atmosphere of 'socialist competition.' Contests are continually organized over whole branches of industry and among Stakhanovites to achieve higher productivity, fastest fulfilment of Plan, lowest cost of production, most complete mastery of new equipment.[21] In 1939, for example, there were contests for tractor and aircraft works. There was competitive inspection of tools and quality of product at heavy-machine factories. Almost all big industrial plants participated in an equipment contest. Winning plants received a Red Banner and several managers and workers were decorated.

Such social recognition must strongly appeal to thousands and tens of thousands of workers and peasants risen from the bottom as a result of the Revolution. 'Hundreds of thousands of workers educated by the Party became talented foremen, engineers, and managers.' [22] In many issues of *Industry* or *Machine-Building* are autobiographies of engineers and managers, peasants and workers by origin, enthusiastically praising their own ascent. In the words of one of the shrewd observers of the new men in management:

> Who are these people . . . ? They belong to that rising class which, in October 1917, took its destiny into its own hands and is building a new socialist society.[23]

These people are imbued with a great passion for success. It may be assumed that this often means not only external success, climbing in the Soviet hierarchy, but also inner success, growth of personality. In autobiographies of Soviet engineers, Stakhan-

[20] *Pravda*, 28 April 1939, has a list of 678 men; in *Industry*, 31 December 1937, are 26 photographs of managers, etc.; in *Machine-Building*, 16 April 1939, there is a list of 188 men.

[21] See Chapter VI.

[22] *Industry*, 21 January 1939.

[23] Y. Il'in, *The Men of the Stalingrad Tractor Works* (Moscow, 1933), p. 3.

ovites, and managers, the expression, 'I am growing,' is common. 'I set my foot on the first step of the ladder,' says Nina Slavikova, a young Moscow Stakhanovite, 'and now I must gather strength, will, and energy to mount to the top.' [24]

All—workers, engineers, managers—have a great desire to learn as a way to advancement: '. . . one must study uninterruptedly and move on and on. And I awfully want to learn and become a highly skilled engineer . . .' [25] This seems typical. Young men and women are keen and persistent. According to engineer Nikolai Gnedin, section head in a chemical factory and ex-shepherd, '. . . the main thing is persistence; everything else—talent, culture—will be added unto you. The main thing is not to retreat and not to languish. Move on!' [26]

Not unlike his equivalent in the capitalist world, the Soviet manager probably has an acute sense of power over men and things. Of this, naturally, we find little in official records, except when gross abuses are disclosed and punished. But we can learn much from novels and short stories. In the novel *Sot'*, by L. Leonov, a writer of sincerity and stature, the Communist Uvad'ev, in charge of the construction of a gigantic paper combine in a dense forest, often displays wanton bossiness.[27] Similar characters are found in other books.

One may doubt the possibility of radically and lastingly reshaping a whole nation in a quarter-century. But much evidence indicates that the character of the younger generation—or at least of its more active representatives—is assuming or has assumed features that did not exist in the pre-revolutionary epoch. One is reminded, in many respects, of the American pioneers. Here, too, are optimism and dynamism, faith in one's individual power and in unlimited national resources. And here is the same love

[24] *Stakhanovites of Moscow, Literary Portraits,* published by Moskovski Rabochii (Moscow, 1936), p. 13.

[25] A young woman engineer in *Industry,* 18 February 1939.

[26] *Stakhanovites of Moscow,* p. 499.

[27] See Chapter IX, below.

for work. Says Aleksei Stakhanov: 'What is moving us? The love of work, which has become for us a source of great human joy.' [28]

Marusya Klekova, a decorated Stakhanovite of nineteen, will devote all her life to work; from ten looms she will go on to twelve, and so on and on. 'There are no limits when one likes one's work.' [29] The chief of a plant section, a former worker, I. Vorob'yev, more than twenty-five years at the Sickle and Hammer Works, says: 'You would no longer recognize our workers. Their relation to work has become quite different. They are moved by a passion for it. Everyone strives to work more and better.' [30] Even if this were true of only a small proportion, the trend of thought of the successful tells much about the accepted scale of values. A novel [31] describes the rise of two foremen: 'We love work,' says one, 'and this love gives us quick wit and skill.'

This joy of work has elements not entirely individualistic. It is a passion to build for the community. A correspondent in the new oil region beyond the Volga, the so-called Second Baku, describes this frame of mind. He chooses clumsy words suited to his administrative ecstasy, but one cannot fail to sense the true substance:

In our country the creation of a new huge oil center begins with the enthusiasm of the Soviet people striving to see and to perceive how, before their very eyes and with the labor of their own hands, the soil is changing and transforming, how despite difficulties and temporary failures a gigantic work is forcing its way and vigorously growing, while the whole country is thrilled by its greatness . . . In the struggle for Soviet oil are manifested the best human feelings reared in our people . . . This feeling of a man striding up and down the construction yard, traversing in waders' boots still uncleared forest paths in joyful consciousness of the importance of his work—this feeling penetrates our engineers . . .[32]

[28] *Industry*, 21 January 1939.
[29] *Stakhanovites of Moscow*, p. 404.
[30] *Industry*, 9 January 1938.
[31] M. Shaginyan, *Two Foremen* (Moscow, 1932).
[32] *Industry*, 6 May 1939.

True, not all Soviet managerial and technical employees are moved by such incentives; many are concerned primarily with salaries and private comforts. No statistics exist on the percentage of enthusiasts, but there is much evidence that the enthusiasm for national construction typifies many workers and employees, technical supervisors and managers, particularly of the younger generation. Many directors of Soviet factories, many members of their staffs are probably convinced that the destiny of country and people depends on their energy. What evidence one has of the conduct of the war with Germany can hardly be reconciled with a picture of mere climbers and hypocrites.

The enthusiasm of construction is bound up with the enthusiasm of youth. Youth sings in the Stakhanovite March: 'We are young because of our tremendous force, we are young because of our faith in victory.' [33]

If we divide the total population of the U.S.S.R. of twenty years and older into two groups, below and above forty years, the younger exceeds the older in numbers by 50 per cent. In the United States the younger group is smaller than the older by 3 per cent, in England and Wales by 15 per cent.[34]

The Soviet population is young. Still greater is the proportion of youth among industrial leaders and the technical personnel. Of 70,000 engineers and technicians employed in heavy industry in 1938, 76.1 per cent were younger than forty.[35] No figures are available for other industries, but biographies of engineers and directors indicate a low average age. This is what one might expect in a country where industry and technical education have developed as rapidly as in modern Russia.[36] The relatively young

[33] *Industry*, 12 January 1939.

[34] Figures for the U.S.S.R. are for 1939, the United States for 1940, England and Wales for 1937. See *Izvestiya*, 29 April 1940; *Statistical Abstract of the United States*, 1941 (Washington, 1942), p. 44; *Statistical Yearbook of the League of Nations*, 1940-41 (Geneva, 1942), Table 3.

[35] *Izvestiya*, 18 and 30 March 1939. For an earlier year (1929) see Chapter IX, note 11.

[36] Compare Chapter IX, on technical education.

also dominate the top of the economic administration. In January 1939, the People's Commissariat for Heavy Industry was split into six smaller Commissariats; the oldest of six new People's Commissars, L. M. Kaganovich, was forty-six;[37] the next in age was forty-four; the others were between thirty-five and thirty-nine.

Youth may have something to do with a vogue for technical novelties. 'The new leading personnel excel in creative power, technical daring, and a love for innovations.'[38] Passion for changes in technology and organization is, indeed, regarded as indispensable in a manager and valuable in a worker. 'The Bolshevik manager is always an innovator.' Stalin said in 1939 that '. . . the sense of the new is a precious quality for every Bolshevik worker . . .'[39]

Personal interests are supposed to merge with collectivist and patriotic ideals in a way peculiar to the Soviet Union. *Industry* published a fictional conversation between visiting American engineers and leading Soviet engineers and managers.[40] To the American's question, 'What do you regard as the chief moving force in your work?' the Russian answers:

> The primary factor is that the man regards the welfare of his country with honesty and devotion; that he always sees the goal for which he is striving, the idea for which he lives, works and creates . . . All our successes can be explained only by the lofty idealism of our people . . . maybe you can grasp what it means to see one's own future in the future of one's country . . .

Russian newspaper correspondents and novelists have often described the great spirit of sacrifice permeating the work of industrialization. Great numbers did or watched the work, and

[37] Born in 1893; at the age of forty-two held a very important post, that of People's Commissar for Transport. It is also worth noting that more than 65 per cent of the members of the Supreme Soviet and more than 90 per cent of the secretaries of local Party committees are, or recently were, under forty. (*Pravda*, 16 January 1938).

[38] A. Kallistov, manager of a new copper-refining plant, in *Industry*, 1 January 1939.

[39] 18th Party Congress, p. 30.

[40] *Industry*, 9 March 1939.

literary exaggerations are unlikely. Here is one vivid description by I. Ehrenburg:

There were 220,000 men at the construction works of Kuznetzk . . . Men felt as in war. They blew up stones, felled trees, stood waistdeep in water, fortifying the dike. Every morning, newspapers brought communiqués about victories and hitches, about a new blast-furnace put into operation, new strata of ore, a subterranean tunnel, a gigantic crane . . . People lived in mud-huts, tiny stoves smoked . . . Bearded Siberians, red partisans and old believers [41] who had never wept were now shedding tears because of the frost . . . Men made haste in laying fire-brick [for the blast furnace]. They set new records every day and lay silently in hospitals with frost-bitten feet or hands . . . They were building a new 'giant.' [42]

Most plant managers are Party members.[43] The Bolsheviks have, through dictatorial methods, liquidated all social forces independent of their government; their Party has become the only manifest social force organizing public opinion. It has sought to produce an atmosphere of creative joy and sacrifice around economic upbuilding. And it has seen to it that leaders of constructive effort feel at one with the Party, remain subject to its discipline while enjoying its privileges. In 1936, 100 per cent of all chiefs of trusts, 97 per cent of all enterprise directors, 82 per cent of all chiefs of construction, 40 per cent of all chief engineers, were Communists.[44] The percentage among engineers, the general role of Communists in industry, has since considerably increased. Party discipline, principles, and directives determine the work of industrial 'commanders,' and 'love of Party' merges with patriotism. This is, at least, the favored and propagandized attitude, although it is difficult to tell how generally and sincerely it is accepted.

[41] Descendants of seventeenth-century non-conformists who, until recently, stubbornly clung to old traditions.

[42] *The Second Day* (Moscow, 1934), pp. 8-9.

[43] See Chapter II.

[44] Central Statistical Office, *U.S.S.R., The Country of Socialism* (Moscow, 1936), p. 94.

The peculiar role of 'intangible' and, *a fortiori*, impersonal incentives in Russian economy must not be exaggerated. Yet it would be wrong to neglect them, to think that the lure of high income and a better apartment, fear of dismissal and punishment, seductions of power, have by themselves been sufficient to make the machinery go round and grow so rapidly. When the Soviet manager must achieve higher labor effort or produce a new technical process, he does not merely give orders. He must explain and justify the innovation, campaign for it, appeal above all to the public interest. One must not forget the tense atmosphere in which industrial work has been done in Russia, the fighting spirit necessary in the Civil War and later to prepare for foreign war. The humblest worker has been made to feel that he is defending an important, dangerous position. Every engineer and director is running a 'battle section,' feels himself a 'commander in the production front.' The plant manager, in fact, must satisfy requirements rather similar to those expected of military commanders.[45] This quasi-military frame of mind accounts for many shortcomings of Soviet industrial management, so often over-impulsive and unmethodical. Instead of systematic, regular work, there are often periods of strain alternating with relaxation; frequent failures, called 'front-breaks,' are followed by spasmodic drives, called 'attacks.' But could the task of rapid industrialization and preparation for a modern war set by Russian political leaders have been fulfilled without this fever of combat and self-sacrifice?

[45] *Industry*, 21 February 1939.

IX

Plant Managers

FROM what environment are heads of Russian factories drawn? How is their rise effected? Can one observe any social consolidation of industrial chiefs—and if so, into what sort of stratum? To these questions final answers cannot now be given. They are too complex, conditions are too unsettled, sources are too often ambiguous. But an attempt must be made to reveal major trends. Since such questions cannot be considered without reference to the working situation, the following account is in part a recapitulation of what has been said in earlier chapters about the position of plant managers.

a. Origins

The beginning of the development is familiar. When, after the Civil War, there began a re-establishment of Russian industry, a certain dualism in management was almost inevitable. Industry was nationalized, but the State did not have at its disposal enough persons both politically trusted and with the special education and experience requisite for the management of industrial enterprises. Thus, a peculiar system was created: at the head of the factory with the rank of manager was a *khozyaistvennik* (economic official), for the most part a Party man, often a former worker. He was assisted by a 'technical director,' often an engineer of considerable experience, but not trusted politically. (In the first years some managers were specialists, with Party commissars beside them.) The situation was further complicated by the 'triangular' relations of manager, Communist Party, and trade-union organs.

As long as the task was merely re-establishment of industry, the system of dual control was fairly acceptable. After this process had been largely completed and the problems of further development and the execution of a great plan of new industrialization arose, the need for a change was intensely felt in government circles. In 1928 there began far-reaching changes in the leading personnel of factory administration which, for the first time, were produced to an important degree by methods familiar later—purges and political trials.

The trial of the engineers of the Shakhty coal mines in the Donbas fields captured public interest.[1] A plenary session of the Central Committee and Central Control Commission of the Communist Party, after hearing Rykov's report 'on the Shakhty affair and practical tasks in combatting errors in economic reconstruction,' resolved as follows:

From the example of the Donbas coal fields, it is evident that in many enterprises the role of the manager has been until now that of a bad commissar . . . Under present conditions it is especially intolerable that economic officials lack knowledge of the productional-technical side of enterprises; that they are often transferred from one kind of work to another; that they are overburdened with tasks utterly alien to the job of production (reports, lectures, trips to the center); that, furthermore, various circumstances transform them from economic leaders into commissars and bad commissars at that, people incapable of assuming genuine responsibility for the work entrusted to them.

It was still not regarded as generally necessary to replace old technical staffs with new men. Emphasis was primarily on the idea of working 'toward the objective of developing a large body of engineers and technicians into active and conscious collaborators in socialist construction.' At the same time, 'particular at-

[1] This first great 'wrecker' trial lasted from 18 May to 5 July 1928 and led to the conviction of forty-seven defendants, almost all engineers, many in high positions; eleven were condemned to death, five executed.

tention' was to be given to the training of 'new staffs of Red specialists.' [2]

The emphasis soon changed, however. Three months later, in a resolution of the plenary session of the Central Committee, July 1928, on 'improvement in the training of new specialists,' [3] a sharper note was discernible. This time it was not the 'appeaser' Rykov, but Molotov who delivered the report. The report called for accelerated training of new specialists, primarily of proletarian origin. The period of study in engineering colleges and technical schools was to be shortened. Far-reaching specialization of study was ordered. It was decided to strengthen the 'workers' nucleus' in engineering colleges and technical schools (*technicums*) [4] to a minimum of 65 per cent of new applicants. This was greatly facilitated by the system of granting scholarships to a majority of students. The Party nucleus was also to be strengthened by commissioning annually for engineering studies at least 1,000 Communists with substantial experience in Party, Soviet, or trade-union activity.[5]

This policy was strongly developed in subsequent years. Along with the education of new specialists, the technical training of old Communist managers was declared one of the most important tasks. For this purpose, factory managers were granted, in addition to annual vacations, special leaves of six weeks to two months 'for the improvement of theoretical qualifications.' [6] Further regulations sought to make it possible for such men to acquire higher technical training without giving up work in factories, through correspondence courses, officially organized private lessons, spe-

[2] *Decisions*, II:269-73.

[3] *Decisions*, II:282-6.

[4] In the Soviet Union a 'technicum' is any intermediate vocational school, whether or not it deals with technology in the narrow sense; thus there are technicums for medicine, pedagogy, and art, as well as for technological education proper.

[5] These decisions were incorporated in substance into government decrees of 27 July and 29 August 1928 and 3 July 1929. *Laws and Ordinances*, 1928:409 and 513; 1929:382.

[6] *Pravda*, 7 September 1928.

cial courses, and other such arrangements. The plenary session of the Central Committee and the Central Control Commission of November 1929 further stressed that the number of engineering colleges with abbreviated terms of study (three years) was to be increased considerably; the nucleus of workers among new students was to be increased to 70 per cent; the number of Communists to be commissioned for engineering studies was to be raised during the next two years from 1,000 to 2,000 and 3,000. The Communist Youth League was given the task of preparing 5,000 students annually for training in engineering colleges and technicums. Further measures were recommended for raising the general level of education, especially in its technical aspects, among capable and diligent workers in order to facilitate their 'promotion' to managerial positions.[7]

In the first half of the first Five Year Plan period, this policy engendered great hostility toward the 'old' engineers. The danger of such a development was soon recognized, however, and Stalin declared on 23 June 1931, before a conference of economic officials:

> During the height of the wrecking movement, we adopted smashing tactics toward the old technical intelligentsia; now, when these intellectuals are turning toward the Soviet power, our policy toward them must be one of conciliation and solicitude. It would be wrong and dialectically incorrect to continue our former policy when conditions have changed. It would now be foolish and unwise to regard almost every expert and engineer of the old schools as an undetected criminal and wrecker.[8]

This 'now' was by no means accidental. Until the day before, practically every engineer of 'the old school' was in constant danger of being regarded as an 'undetected criminal.'

[7] *Decisions,* II:367-74. Compare the decrees of the Central Executive Committee and the Council of People's Commissars, 1 January 1930 and 21 June 1931, respectively. *Laws and Ordinances,* 1930:65, and 1931:288.

[8] J. Stalin, *Problems of Leninism* (11th ed., Moscow, 1939), p. 344; English edition published under title *Leninism* (New York, 1933), p. 440.

The principles of this 'cadre policy,' first formulated in 1928-9, remained almost unchanged until the mid-thirties. To be sure, they were relaxed in some degree by the restriction of 'promotion' of workers into administrative offices. There was a serious shortage of qualified hands resulting from the rapid growth of industry. Consequently, through decision of the Central Committee of the Party 'regarding measures for the planned supply of manpower to the national economy and for combatting labor turnover,'[9] the promotion of workers into administrative offices was forbidden for two years. But this did not apply to promotion of a worker into administrative offices within his industry and more especially within an enterprise. Although the Party decision was dictated by labor-market conditions rather than by any change in the cadre policy, this turned out to be, in effect, a forerunner of a coming change in policy.

Although the principal social ideas of the cadre policy remained unchanged until the mid-thirties, real education of new cadres was greatly modified as early as 1932. The government[10] acknowledged that the system of accelerated education for engineers and technicians had failed, that enthusiasm for great numbers of engineering colleges and technical schools, for hundreds of thousands of students, and for extreme specialization of education had lowered the level of technical training. Orders were issued to lengthen the period of education, revise curricula, and introduce a general system of strict entrance examinations. This last measure limited, in effect, the influx of workers (and their children) into colleges and technical schools. The section of the decree devoted to 'recruiting for the engineering colleges and technical schools' did not mention a 'workers' nucleus.' While regulations on this point were not formally revoked, they were pushed into the background and little by little forgotten.

[9] *Pravda*, 22 October 1930.

[10] Decree of the Central Executive Committee, 19 September 1932, *Laws and Ordinances*, 1932:409.

The cadre policy as introduced in 1928-9 greatly influenced the composition of leading industrial cadres in subsequent years. The old 'technical intelligentsia' [11] lost its standing in the factories. Management fell into the hands of Communist economic officials who had had brief technical education. Increasing numbers of 'Red specialists' were advanced to leading positions. But, for the most part, these were not young persons who had gone directly from high school or technical school to an engineering college. Most of them had a record of years of work and struggle when they entered colleges for brief training. Socially, they were almost the same type as other Communist *khozyaistvenniki* who had had some technical education. They did not as a rule regard themselves simply as technicians, but considered technical work a continuation of their previous activity, influenced chiefly by social and political motives. Although their social and political ideas had changed considerably since the beginning of the Revolution, its first years continued to represent to them not history but their own intimate past. This trait of the industrial chiefs of the early thirties is of great importance for an understanding of the social development of the Soviet Union. Before these chiefs are more concretely characterized, some idea of the extent of the phenomenon may be given.

The number of students in higher institutions and technicums—especially those for industrial training—increased tremendously

[11] The average age of this group was lower than might be assumed. Even at the beginning of this period, engineers and technicians, both graduate and 'practical' (that is, with incomplete specialized training), who had begun professional activity before the Revolution, comprised only a minority of all engineers and technicians. In January 1929 the Central Statistical Office, in collaboration with the Supreme Council of National Economy, conducted an inquiry in twenty-five of the largest industrial plants (employing more than 300,000 workers) and in several industrial administration bodies. Of the 8,995 engineers and technicians covered, only 30.7 per cent had begun professional activity before 1918 (in industrial plants only 28.9 per cent of 6,006). Of 3,446 graduate engineers, only 34.7 per cent, and of 1,487 graduate technicians only 34.2 per cent had been graduated before 1917. See S. Kheinman, 'The Composition of the Cadres of Engineers and Technicians in the U.S.S.R.,' *Economic Review*, December 1929, pp. 102ff.

during the period of the first Five Year Plan, as is evident from the following figures: [12]

Engineering Colleges Training for Industry and Transportation

	ADMISSIONS		GRADUATIONS	
Year	*Total*	*Industry*	*Total*	*Industry*
1928	16,800	.....	8,900	.....
1929	22,900	.....	11,000	.....
1930	78,400	.....	20,800	.....
1931	88,600	.....	18,800	.....
1932	114,500	93,300	17,100	14,500
1933	55,800	43,700	7,900	6,100
1934	53,300	42,600	18,900	14,900
1935	49,100	39,000	37,200	29,600
1936	34,600	26,500	35,800	29,200
1937	41,000	31,800	34,600	27,600
1938	54,200	43,500	31,300	25,400

Technicums Training for Industry and Transportation

	ADMISSIONS		GRADUATIONS	
Year	*Total*	*Industry*	*Total*	*Industry*
1928	17,700	.....	6,800	.....
1929	25,100	.....	8,300	.....
1930	165,900	.....	14,000	.....
1931	126,300	.....	29,600	.....
1932	177,800	124,000	46,700	33,600
1933	108,600	77,600	52,600	31,400
1934	99,300	70,800	36,700	29,200
1935	91,000	65,700	45,400	31,900
1936	79,000	58,800	40,900	27,900
1937	78,200	58,100	37,600	27,100
1938	93,100	69,200	44,100	30,500

The import of these figures may be better appreciated if it is remembered that in 1927-8, immediately before the beginning of the first Five Year Plan, only 20,200 engineers were employed in all Soviet industry.[13] Most newly admitted students left colleges

[12] See Central Statistical Office, *Cultural Construction in the U.S.S.R.* (Moscow, 1940), pp. 111-12. In the following tables the figures for industry include the construction industry, those for transportation include communications. Dots indicate years for which data are lacking.

[13] See Gosplan, *Five Year Plan for the Development of the National Economy of the U.S.S.R.* (Moscow, 1929), 1:76.

and technicums after one or two years of study, and never finished their education. Hence the great difference between the number admitted and the number graduated. After 1932 the number of new admissions was no longer so tremendous, while graduations increased. These figures indicate improved training of freshmen, owing to changed principles of admission.

Of interest also are figures regarding the social origin of students. In 1928-33, the proportion of former manual workers (and their children) among students increased rapidly. In 1933 there began a reverse development.[14]

Percentage of Manual Workers (and Their Children) Among Students Training for Industry and Transportation

	1928	1931	1933	1935	1938
Higher institutions	38.3	61.9	64.6	59.8	43.5 for industry 48.8 for transportation
Technicums	38.5	60.1	62.2	51.7	41.0 for industry 42.8 for transportation

Inasmuch as the percentage of workers in the population increased greatly from 1928 to 1938, the proportion of workers (and their children) among students of higher institutions and technicums appears to have been in 1938 relatively about the same as in 1928. On the other hand, the percentage of salaried employees (or their children) among students grew considerably. The proportion of peasants and their children remained small.

[14] See Central Statistical Office, *Socialist Construction in the U.S.S.R.* (Moscow, 1934), p. 410, ibid. (1936), p. 576, and *Cultural Construction in the U.S.S.R.* (Moscow, 1940), p. 114. The percentage of manual workers (and their children) among students of *all*—not only industrial, etc.—higher educational institutions and technicums was:

	1928	1931	1933	1935	1938
Higher institutions	25.4	46.6	50.3	45.0	33.9
Technicums	25.8	42.6	41.5	31.7	27.1

Social Origins of Students in Higher Institutions[15]

	ALL HIGHER INSTITUTIONS, 1938		TRAINING FOR INDUSTRY, 1938		TRAINING FOR INDUSTRY, 1934	
	Thousands	*Per cent*	*Thousands*	*Per cent*	*Thousands*	*Per cent*
Manual workers and their children	181	33.9	50	43.5	94	61.2
Salaried employees and specialists and their children	225	42.2	52	45.4	48	31.1
Peasants and their children	115	21.6	11	9.6	11	7.5
Others	12	2.3	2	1.5	..	0.2
TOTAL	533	100.0	115	100.0	153	100.0

Formerly students classified as children of salaried employees were largely children of medium- and lower-salaried employees, in a material and social situation comparable to that of manual workers. Now what was meant by children of salaried employees was increasingly children of the higher-salaried.[16] The lower-salaried appear to have lost the opportunity to give their children

[15] *Cultural Construction in the U.S.S.R.*, pp. 114, 127; Central Statistical Office, *Cultural Construction in the U.S.S.R. in Figures, from the 6th to the 7th Soviet Congresses*, 1930-34 (Moscow, 1935), pp. 40, 56. Absolute figures for 1934 had to be estimated on the basis of published percentages given in the last column, and the following considerations: in 1934 there were 199,000 students training for either industry or transportation; applying to 1934 the 1938 ratio of 'industry' to 'transportation' (115:35), the number training for industry in 1934 can be estimated at 153,000. The number of students in all higher institutions in 1934 was 417,000.

[16] According to V. Molotov, *The Third Five Year Plan*, Address to the 18th Party Congress (Moscow, 1939), pp. 44-5, in January 1937 there were 450,000 chiefs of administrative bodies and institutions of health and culture; 350,000 chiefs and assistant chiefs of industrial enterprises, sections, and departments; 250,000 other engineers and architects; 132,000 physicians; 80,000 agronomists; 80,000 college professors. To these 1,342,000 people in leading positions or with college education might be added sections of some other groups: 822,000 economists and statisticians; 969,000 teachers; 297,000 journalists, librarians, etc.; some specialist groups of lesser importance; and 1,550,000 'other groups of intelligentsia' (see Introduction to the present book, p. xxiii). One may roughly estimate the number of higher-salaried employees and specialists at 2,500,000 to 3,000,000. As in the United States, almost all such persons try to give their children a higher education. Of the total of less than 250,000 children of salaried employees in institutions of higher learning, few can come from the lower strata.

a higher education. Significantly, in 1938 the official statistical rubric was for the first time 'children of salaried employees and specialists.'

b. Social Types

Before proceeding to developments that began in 1936-7, we must describe the earlier type, or rather types, of industrial chiefs.

Soviet *belles-lettres* provide one of the best sources for the study of social development and changes in Soviet Russia. Literary activity has become a favored profession and, however modest its artistic value generally, literary production has been quantitatively great. In any case, its value as a source of knowledge of modern Russia is great, inasmuch as the element of fiction in many works, compared to the amount of straight reporting, is minor. Although exposition is often mutilated by conscious or semi-conscious adaptation to the official political ideology, an attentive reader with some knowledge of the country can easily discern the true face of the people under the official cosmetics.

During the last twenty years, and especially since the beginning of the broad industrialization policy, numerous novels have depicted industrial enterprises. In many, industrial chiefs are central characters. The well-known novel of Fedor Gladkov, *Cement* (1924),[17] is a pioneer in this type of literature. Gleb Chumalov, former worker in a cement plant, comes home in 1921 after the Civil War and finds the plant long since closed. Through his energy and initiative, the plant is set in motion and Chumalov becomes its manager. Now begins his new psychological development, somewhat hazily presented. Clearly shown, however, is another representative of the new rising stratum of Communist administrators and managers, the chairman of the executive committee of the local Soviet, Bad'in. Also a former worker, he is strenuous, cocksure, hard, and somewhat disdainful of 'romantics of the Revolution,' as he calls Chumalov in a friendly way. Dur-

[17] Novels are cited according to date of first publication, which in some cases was in serial form.

ing the years of industrial recovery, many industrial chiefs were drawn from such human material.

At this time factory managers were chosen chiefly from among workers who had played an active role in the local labor movement, often in the same factories, since the beginning of the Revolution or even before. It is characteristic that only seldom were they former leading members of the labor movement. In the beginning of the twenties the old leaders won higher posts—in general administration, in the economic, political, and military machines, etc. To manage factories became the task of those former corporals of the labor movement who, like Bad'in, were ready to sacrifice the special and immediate labor interests to 'the factory,' the 'national economy,' 'the State.' Chumalov, lacking this hardness, also lacked inner firmness to oppose the dominant trend. He let the current carry him along and never became a genuine manager. We shall meet him again at the beginning of the thirties in Gladkov's *Energy*, as Assistant Manager during the construction of Dnepr dam, where his special task was to maintain good relations between the administration and the workers. Here he seems to be more of an official than a leader.

Gladkov long remained rather isolated in his attempt to make an industrial enterprise the center of a novel, but approximately since 1928-9 authors have taken a growing interest in industrial plants, especially those in construction. Typical subjects have been a great paper factory in Leonid Leonov's *Sot'* (1929), the gigantic Dnepr electric power station in Gladkov's *Energy* (2 vols., 1932-8), the Magnitogorsk plant in Valentin Katayev's *Time, Forward!* (1932), the Kuznetzk plant in Il'ya Ehrenburg's *The Second Day* (1933), the Stalingrad tractor plant in Yakov Il'in's *The Great Conveyer* (1934). This choice of themes was not accidental. At this time it was semi-officially suggested that recognized writers study the construction of large plants and depict them fictionally with some changes of names. In most of the above-named novels, we see managers of plants in construction and in production, at work and at home. The exposition is only formally fictional. Aside from that of Ehrenburg, which happens to be of no importance for our purposes, the sole piece of pure fiction is that of Leonov; nevertheless, as the work of a master, it is of great value for a knowledge of modern Russia.

Different from Chumalov and more like Bad'in, is Uvad'yev, manager of a projected paper factory (*Sot'*), a former worker, later foreman of a paper factory. The factory is being constructed in economically virgin country, and Uvad'yev is alien, almost hostile, to the peasant environment. He does not consider people as such; for him they are only material for the gigantic process of industrial recovery, only 'man power' for the factory and its construction. When he finds it necessary to proceed as a 'hard-hearted *khozyain*' (the word corresponds almost exactly to 'boss'), he does so without inner conflict.

At the beginning of the first Five Year Plan, it was deemed an asset in a Communist manager to be a 'hard khozyain.' Zharkov, in *Leningrad* by Mikhail Chumandrin (1932), a former worker, later secretary of a Communist factory cell, now manager of an industrial trust, tells a friend with some defiance and characteristic exaggeration, 'Between us we know we cannot be frightened even if the bones should crack,' even if the worker 'has it three times as bad as in the old days.' In *Morning Begins in Moscow* by Leonid Ovalow (1936), Yartzev, a worker during the first Five Year Plan, is so captivated by his later managerial role that he does not shrink from conflicts with the most devoted workers; the author adds conciliatingly: 'This was overdoing it. Yartzev understood this, but he was seized by the exciting universal love of the machine . . . A young khozyain!'

Ignatov, manager of a tractor plant (*The Great Conveyer*), a former fitter and sailor, had distinguished himself on the Civil War front; later a Party and Che-ka worker, he was transferred to economic work at the end of the NEP, first as construction manager of a tractor plant and then as plant manager. He is resolute, rough, opinionated, extremely self-confident. 'Soviet-Chicago will be created here and I, Ignatov, will construct this

Chicago.' The word 'I' occupies an important place in his vocabulary. He has a powerful will, inexhaustible energy, is without personal interest, knows nothing but his work. An engineer in the plant characterizes him as 'a talented barbarian.' He belongs to the type of primitive revolutionary adventurer which rose to industrial leadership. He does not understand that a modern complicated plant cannot be directed by brutal methods; he fails and is replaced by a former mechanic, Barkov, who had worked in the economic administration since 1918.

During the twelve years he worked in six provinces, held ten positions. He was chairman of a provincial Economic Council, chief of municipal enterprises, manager of various plants. He was accustomed to consider himself an organizer and administrator, devoted to political and administrative affairs; technical affairs were the province of engineers.

He became a typical man of routine, without personal will, anxious only for the favor of superior authorities. 'Let it cost what it may, the tractors must be constructed.' Finally, he also fails.

From Moscow comes as an interim manager, the chief of the country's automobile and tractor industry, Seliverstov, an old Bolshevik and an outstanding engineer. He succeeds in regularizing work by eliminating the feverish speed-up (*shturmovshchina*, the 'storming-craze') and creating order. But his personality remains indistinct: Soviet authors in general have not succeeded in portraying outstanding engineers as old Bolsheviks—e.g. Baleyev, constructor of the Dnepr hydroelectric station in *Energy*, the assistant manager of Magnitogorsk, Nalbandov in *Time, Forward!* They are schematic, not living men.

Younger engineers are presented more convincingly. Their rise to leading positions in plants began with the Five Year Plan, but in none of the novels of recognized writers do we see a young engineer as plant manager. Perhaps this is to be explained by the predominant interest of writers in large enterprises, whereas young engineers began their rise as managers in medium-sized and smaller enterprises. But in almost every novel we meet young engineers as chiefs of sections or in similar posts in large plants. Mere boys of fifteen to seventeen at the beginning of the Revolution, they were carried along by the current, later passed through the school of the Young Communist League, participated in the late twenties in the struggle inside the Communist Party (Stalin's fight against right and left 'deviations'), and finally accepted Stalin's policy, less out of political motives than because Stalin became, for them, a symbol of the new order with its prospect of great industrial expansion. Some came from a worker milieu, many from peasant homes, but most of them from the urban middle classes, although often before entering college they had spent one or two years as manual workers. Incidentally, during the twenties and the first half of the thirties, this was the natural road to higher education for middle-class youth.

These young engineers were a restless element, inclined toward experimentation, record-breaking, speed-up, 'storming.' They brought *élan* into the plants, a sense that people somehow become embodied in the gigantic recovery of the new revolutionary country through work in which they submerge themselves completely. Confident of advancement, but largely not conscious careerists, they saw their rise as a natural consequence of the development of the young country. Hence their social optimism and blindness toward new social inequalities. We meet these young engineers in almost all novels portraying industrial plants at the beginning of the first Five Year Plan. In *Time, Forward!* such an engineer, Morgul'yes, is the center of action; in *The Great Conveyer* there is a whole group of such engineers. At the end of the first Five Year Plan, many will become plant managers.

Many novelists show special interest in 'old' engineers in leading posts. This is probably to be explained by the complex situation faced by such men in plants. In *Cement* we see the prerevolutionary leading engineer, Kleist, who becomes technical director of the re-established plant. He is alien, perhaps hostile, to the new political system, but his interest in the work outweighs everything else and he is loyal and tireless. This trait is peculiar to most important engineers in novels depicting the period of industrial recovery. The feeling that they are playing an active part in economic rebuilding, that they are the real creative force of industrial recovery, influenced many of them. This spirit found expression in the words of engineer Gabrukh in Sergei Semenov's *Natal'ya Tarpova* (1928): 'The men of October, at the head of the country, began to do the same work, practically, that the non-Party engineer, Gabrukh, would do in their place: they are building the country up anew.' This alone, and no assumption that the country is developing 'in a socialist corset,' is of interest to Gabrukh. He is convinced that 'tomorrow will show them [i.e. the Communists] for whom they have worked.'

The idea that, in a country with nationalized industry, economic and especially industrial progress must increase their social importance was widespread among engineers and softened the 'anti-Bolshevism' of the older men. A singular kind of Soviet patriotism sprang up in this milieu, with special emphasis on the dignity of labor. 'Only work, only the accumulation of values, can save Russia,' says the non-Party engineer, Forst, in Pilnyak's *Machines and Wolves* (1925), and he gives his hand to the Communist, Lebedoukha, with the words, 'we must travel the same path.' Another engineer in the same novel, Roschislavski, welcomes 'the black hand, hard and steely,' which could 'grip Russia and the Russian muzhik, bring order out of the Russian chaos'; this hand has seized everything by the throat; 'it will build—do you hear?—build!'

It was this feeling and this mood that produced a certain unrest in leading Soviet circles and led to the 'wrecker' trials. After 1929, the 'wrecker' engineers were also portrayed in novels, but they were largely caricatures, not living men. An exception was one in *The Great Conveyer*. Stavrovski, senior engineer, later assistant manager of a tractor plant, is a convicted wrecker. He was the alleged head of wrecking work in the whole automobile and tractor industry. Even now in the plant he is under the special supervision of GPU agents. But, while not concealing his disapproval of the fanaticism of the prevailing speed-up, he works with devotion. Before the court he 'confessed'; the author does not dare doubt his guilt. But when the chief of the Supreme Council of National Economy, Ordzhonikidze, visits the tractor plant, he expresses the greatest confidence in Stavrovski and guarantees his unconditional and complete amnesty.[18]

The wrecker trials left bitterness in leading engineering circles. *Energy* presents a highly trained and energetic engineer, Kryazhich, directing the construction of the Dnepr electric station. He was nearly involved in a wrecker trial. In a conversation with the leader of the local Party organization, he says bitterly:

> If I am humiliated, if I have no equal rights with you, if at any moment I can be crushed and destroyed—what shall I call this? . . . If anyone can push his dirty hand under my nose and boast of his proletarian origin as if it were a Masonic symbol, then I have a right to protest and defend myself . . . If socialism is built on such filth, on such arrogance—I reject such a socialism.

Of course, it is possible that among the engineers were some real wreckers, but they were undoubtedly few. And wrecking as a mass phenomenon involving a large number of engineers, such as was officially alleged during the first Five Year Plan, surely did not belong to the world of realities. In the mid-thirties the question had evidently lost its importance. The dualism, manager-technical manager, had, on the whole been surmounted. New problems of industrial management arose.

c. Later Developments

The mid-thirties must have appeared to factory managers as a brilliant period. A great number of gigantic new industrial plants

[18] The mechanism of the 'confessions' of the wrecker engineers is shown in the book of a former Yugoslavian Communist, A. Ciliga, *The Russian Enigma* (London, 1940). Ciliga had an opportunity to become acquainted with many wreckers in a Leningrad prison.

were already in operation, others were in construction, and the immediate future promised tremendous industrial expansion. The names of the managers of the larger plants were among the best known in the country.

There were no more Ignatovs and Uvad'yevs, no more Morgul'yes, or the like, such as we met some years earlier. Early in the thirties arose a type of plant chief who combined the traits of both groups. The position of these managers appeared brilliant, their future secure. But at the end of 1936 the situation was painfully altered. From the last months of 1936 until well into 1938 a change, broader and more radical than in 1928-9, took place in the leading industrial personnel. Most important industrial chiefs were replaced by new men. They were not only new individuals, but also new types, men of new backgrounds, experiences, and attitudes, who probably even represented a new social stratum, one not consolidated but in process of formation.

This turnover of industrial chiefs came about by means of the great 'purge.' It began with the Zinov'yev-Kamenev trial in August 1936, reached its highest point in the P'yatakov-Radek trial in January 1937, and led to the elimination of the larger part of leading officials in the State administration and the Communist Party. Not hundreds, but many thousands were victims of this purge. In every even moderately important enterprise and office, in leading circles of the government, and in the Central Committee of the Communist Party, the purge was felt. The replacing of chiefs of industrial plants by new men was only one aspect of this social upheaval. Its broader aspects—historical roots, inner motives, sociological significance—cannot be analyzed in this study. Here we are interested only in the way in which the purge operated in industrial plants, how it affected the formation of a new industrial leadership.

As in 1928-9, the losing group was politically discredited. But now defamation was practiced with greater ruthlessness. As we have seen, wreckers sentenced in 1928-9 could sometimes continue to work in plants, although under special supervision. Often officials did not take convictions seriously. But in 1936-8 accusations led to much more serious punishment. Furthermore, the charges now were raised not only against engineers, as in 1928-9, but almost everywhere.

The new industrial chiefs were young men, often scarcely out of school, with a better and more systematic education than most of the 'Red specialists' who preceded them. They were more interested in their profession, less in political problems. Most of them leaned toward authoritarian thinking: the supreme leadership (Stalin and those closest to him) decides on right and wrong; what it decides is incontrovertible, absolute. Thus, complete devotion to Stalin. It would be undue simplification to explain this devotion merely by the fact that the system represented by Stalin made possible the rise of these people. It had deeper roots. They had been young Communists who ripened intellectually as the opposition within the Communist Party was being broken and defamed and a Stalin cult systematically developed. Stalin was, for them, the embodiment of economic progress and a strengthened international position. They accepted as natural the fact that industrialization and rearmament were dearly paid for, that the bulk of the toiling masses remained in dire want. They were educated to the idea that a society with a developed industry and without a capitalist class corresponds, *ipso facto*, to the ideal of a 'classless society,' and that to strive for social equality would be mere 'petty bourgeois leveling.' [19] The interest of the new men was less in social problems than in a strong State to build a national economy.

Not only did the influx of workers and workers' children into collegiate institutions fall off markedly after 1933; promotion of

[19] *Soviet Labor Law*, a college textbook published by the People's Commissariat for Justice (Moscow, 1939), describes the tendency to equalize wages of skilled and unskilled workers as a feature of capitalist countries, and emphasizes the socialist character of wage differentials; 'petty bourgeois egalitarianism in wage policies is the worst enemy of socialism.' Incidentally, neither 'leveling' nor 'egalitarianism' can render the contemptuous, slangy sound of the Russian word used, ***uravnilovka.***

workers directly from the bench into administrative positions was almost stopped in the second half of the thirties. Outstanding workers were now given higher wages, bonuses, and the like, and in their social and material position were elevated high above the majority of workers, almost to the level of higher ranks of plant employees and engineers. But they remained manual workers. By this time relatively few of these favored workers saw the way open to higher education, saw a prospect of rising to industrial leadership. Lost was the idea of putting management into the hands of men rising from the working class and bound to labor, formulated at the end of the twenties. The order to assure a workers' nucleus in colleges and technical schools had been forgotten.

Through a decree of the Council of People's Commissars of 2 October 1940, scholarships were limited to outstanding students, those with not less than one-third 'excellent' examination marks and no marks below 'good.' This measure, while tending to raise the level of college education, was bound to have a social effect. As there were no scholarships in secondary schools, the poor had a relatively small chance of getting 'excellent' marks. Hence the new restriction on college scholarships diminished their chances of obtaining a higher education. This tendency was strengthened by the simultaneous introduction of fees in secondary schools (8th, 9th, and 10th grades of elementary schools), technicums, and colleges (fees range between 150 and 200 roubles a year in high schools, 300 to 500 in colleges).[20]

The social effect of these measures is further illuminated by a simultaneous decree of the Presidum of the Supreme Council, introducing compulsory vocational education of boys from fourteen to seventeen. After training of six months (for boys of sixteen and seventeen, to teach them the tasks of a 'semi-skilled' worker), or of two years (for boys of fourteen and fifteen, to teach them the tasks of a 'skilled' worker), young men are bound

[20] Decrees of 2 and 12 October 1940; *Laws and Ordinances*, 1940:637, 676.

for four years as manual workers in enterprises chosen by a special authority. This compulsory vocational training (and consequent compulsory labor) is not general: 800,000 to 1,000,000 boys are 'mobilized' annually for vocational schools, but students of high schools and colleges are tacitly exempt.[21] Whatever the motives of these decrees, they would, in effect, emphasize the social-privilege aspect of higher education. Future industrial chiefs would grow up from school days with a feeling of social superiority.

It is characteristic of recent developments that young engineers are increasingly promoted not only in industrial plants but everywhere, and especially in Communist Party offices and general administration. The important role of engineers and technicians was brought out directly by the last general election campaign within the Communist Party (1938). 'A new favorable phenomenon must be especially mentioned,' said the Moscow Party Secretary, Ugarov, at the Moscow Party conference: 'A great number of engineers and technicians work in the Party.' [22] Similar remarks were made at the Congress of the Communist Party of the Ukraine by its First Secretary, Khrushchov.[23] Newspapers published frequent reports of the election of engineers and technicians to secretaryships of Party organizations in plants.

Some engineers even entered the government of the U.S.S.R. There are today twenty-five People's Commissariats for industry,[24] many headed by young engineers, some of whom rose to these positions directly from the office of plant manager. Engineers today constitute approximately one-third of the Council of People's Commissars. And although its members have, on the

[21] *Izvestiya,* 3 October 1940. The census of January 1939 showed for the entire Soviet Union 13,336,000 persons of ten to fourteen years of age and 15,124,000 of fifteen to nineteen (*Izvestiya,* 29 April 1940). Thus we can estimate the number of boys and girls of fourteen to seventeen at about 12,000,000, the number of boys at about 6,000,000.

[22] *Pravda,* 31 May 1938.

[23] *Pravda,* 16 July 1938.

[24] See Chapter I.a.

whole, less political power than English or even American Cabinet members, this development strengthens considerably the social consciousness of engineers in leading positions in industrial plants.

The social process described above is far from completed. It was in full tide when the German-Russian war began. The war may deflect it, but a knowledge of social change in the last years before the war can, perhaps, facilitate an understanding of coming events.

PART II

MANAGEMENT OF COLLECTIVE FARMS

X

The Kolkhoz: A New Production Form [1]

THE *kolkhoz*, or collective farm, is a new form of productive organization in agriculture. Before embarking on a study of the management of kolkhozes, it is necessary briefly to review their development and to describe their peculiar structure.

The first voluntary kolkhozes were organized in the early days of the Revolution, when the land belonging to the rural gentry, monasteries, churches, etc., was nationalized and turned over to the peasants for cultivation. Rapid liquidation of large agricultural enterprises and division of confiscated lands among the peasants proceeded simultaneously with a parceling even of small peasant holdings. Two circumstances were chiefly instrumental in this process: the economic collapse of the cities and the possibility of obtaining an allotment of land attracted urban elements which had not yet lost their ties with the village. In the redistributions of land, which during the Revolution were repeated almost yearly, they too received plots, according to the number of workers or heads in a family depending on the district. The Soviet government, which, to feed the cities, systematically extracted grain and other agricultural products from the village, was particularly heavy on the owners of larger farms. This policy contributed to subdividing larger farms, owned by large families, into smaller independent holdings.

This process of dividing agricultural enterprises that even

[1] For further details on kolkhozes see A. Yugow, 'The Collectivization of Agriculture in the U.S.S.R.' in the *International Labor Review* (September 1932), vol. 26, no. 3, and *Russia's Economic Front for War and Peace: An Appraisal of the Three Five Year Plans* (New York, 1942).

theretofore had been on the whole extremely small resulted in a rapid decrease in the amounts of goods which farms could spare for city needs, i.e. a decrease in agricultural production for the market. Petty farmsteads, poor both in capital and in technical equipment, were barely able to provide minimum subsistence for peasants and their families.

As a result, the leaders of Soviet economy and, to some extent, the active elements of the peasantry began seeking an organizational form of production which would allow small peasants to avail themselves of the advantages of large-scale enterprise: rational crop rotation, machines, processing and storage facilities, and direct sale to city markets. There followed a trend toward co-operation. Co-operatives in home industries, credit, and marketing had existed throughout the country even before the Revolution of 1917, and were particularly widespread in the Ukraine, northern Russia, the Urals, and Siberia. On the outbreak of the war in 1914 there were about 4,700 co-operative societies in Russia for the processing and marketing of agricultural products.[2] In addition, there were approximately 11,000 rural consumer co-operatives. The total co-operative membership at that time was more than 2,000,000 persons.

As early as 1918 there appeared the first collective farms with various degrees of pooling of property, implements, and labor. Many of these were established on nationalized large estates, which local government agencies placed at the disposal of the peasants for collective cultivation.

These early kolkhozes generally took the form of simple co-operation for the joint acquisition and use of complex machines (multiple metal plows, reaping machines, etc.). They were called 'societies for joint land cultivation' (*toz*). Land remained the property of individual owners who were toz members, and the output of each parcel belonged to its owner. Livestock and the

[2] A. Lozovy, *Agricultural Co-operation and Its Significance* (Moscow, 1923).

smaller implements also remained outside co-operative ownership. Pastures, however, were often used in common.

Another method of collective farming was the agricultural 'artel.' Here the land, heavy tools and machines, farm buildings, and work animals were held in common. Individual land holdings were lumped together, subdivided into fields according to crop, and worked collectively. The total output was divided among members according to either labor, or shares, or the number of workers, or the number of consumers.

There were, finally, agricultural 'communes,' which organized collectively not only the production, but also members' consumption. All implements, machines, livestock, and buildings were owned by the commune; members lived in communal homes, with communal kitchens, nurseries, etc. Most of such agricultural communes were organized by workers who had come from the cities.

According to the Agrarian Institute of the U.S.S.R., collective farms were composed mainly of the poorer rural elements. In particular, the poorest peasants joined the communes, since they had almost no private property to begin with. In 1928, 70.9 per cent of the membership of communes were landless peasants, 74.3 per cent owned no horses. Of toz members, only 29.4 per cent were landless and 48.1 per cent horseless.[8]

Although, from the outset, the kolkhozes had government support (tax exemptions, credits, subsidies), they were but slowly adopted into the agricultural economy of the country. Despite the advantages of large-scale mechanized agriculture, in the majority of cases the kolkhozes did not efficiently organize production. This was partly because of lack of experience in the leadership, but chiefly because of internal frictions and conflicts arising as a result of unfamiliar forms and methods. Of the various forms of collective organization, the communes proved the least viable. Struggling with problems of production and complexities of

[8] People's Commissariat for Agriculture, *The Kolkhozes of the U.S.S.R.* (Moscow, 1929), p. 40.

communal living, they frequently survived only by virtue of government aid. Gradually they died out.

The most widespread and successful of all kolkhoz forms was the toz. In 1927, communes accounted for 9.0, tozes for 42.9, and artels for 48.1 per cent of all kolkhozes; by 1929, communes had dwindled to 6.2, artels to 33.6, while the tozes had increased to 60.2 per cent.

During the first years of the Revolution, the number of kolkhozes of all kinds increased. During the NEP the increase was first slowed down, then, as private farming regained a foothold, the number of kolkhozes began to diminish. In 1918 there were 1,600 kolkhozes, comprising 0.1 per cent of all farms; in 1921 there were 16,000 kolkhozes, comprising 0.9 per cent; in 1925 there were 21,900, comprising 1.2 per cent; and in 1927 there were 14,800, comprising 0.8 per cent.[4]

Thus we see that the kolkhozes of 1918-28, organized along the lines of voluntary co-operation, embraced but an insignificant percentage of the peasantry and never played a large role in the rural economy.

If, at this same time, agricultural production was restored to a certain degree, improvement was slow because the process of the subdivision of farming units continued during the years of the NEP. This was a result both of the natural increase in population, and of the 'anti-kulak' policy of the government. Before the Revolution, the annual percentage of farms subdivided did not exceed 1.7 per cent. During 1917-28, it ranged from 2.3 per cent to 3.5 per cent. The number of individual farms rose from 18 million in 1917 to 25 million in 1928.[5]

The relative rehabilitation of rural economy was undoubtedly aided by the abolition (in 1921) of the compulsory requisitioning

[4] Central Statistical Office, *The Kolkhozes in the Second Five Year Plan* (Moscow, 1939), p. 1, and *Socialist Agriculture of the U.S.S.R.* (Moscow, 1939), p. 42.

[5] P. Lyashchenko, *Russian Grain Farming* (Moscow, 1927), p. 16. *The Kolkhozes of the U.S.S.R.*, p. 44.

of farm products (which meant, as Lenin explained, that 'the peasant must surrender to the government every pood of grain not essential for the maintenance of his family, for cattle feed or for seed' [6]) and its replacement by fixed levies in kind. But the government did not go so far as to adopt a definite policy of encouraging the economically strong peasant elements. During the last years of the NEP, general agricultural production and, particularly, production for the market remained stagnant or decreased. In 1927, despite the relatively high total yield of grain, the countryside gave the city only 37 per cent of the grain usually marketed in pre-Soviet days. In spite of very severe government decrees, the marketing of animal products and of agricultural raw materials needed by industry decreased. In 1926-7 the ratio of marketed agricultural goods to total output was, in flax, 66 per cent of the corresponding pre-war ratio (1913); in leather, 82 per cent; in poultry, 58 per cent; in wool, 46 per cent.[7]

This decrease in production for the market had its chief roots in the size of farm units and the structure of agrarian economy. Even before the First World War, peasant holdings were incapable of providing subsistence to owners, who were compelled to go to cities to work or beg. The great mass of small peasant holdings had been operated on a level close to primitive subsistence. Production for the market had been carried on chiefly by the middle and large peasant farms and by landed estates. Lack of space prevents citation of detailed data on the extent of market production, which varied with crop, region, acreage, availability of livestock, etc.[8] On the basis of his studies of agricultural production over a long period in many regions of pre-Soviet Russia, Kondrat'yev established that for all regions and crops the marketed proportion of output of landed estates and large peasant

[6] V. I. Lenin, *Collected Works* (Moscow, 1932), xv:332. A pood is an old Russian measure of weight, equivalent to 36.113 pounds.

[7] N. Kondrat'yev, *The Grain Market* (Moscow, 1927), p. 14; *Economic Life*, 3 May 1927.

[8] N. Oganovski, *Outlines of Russian Economics* (Moscow, 1923), pp. 105-6.

farms was considerably higher (2 to 3½ times) than that of middle and small peasant farms.[9] The figures of the Central Statistical Office of the U.S.S.R. give an approximate idea of the relation of market production to size of enterprise. Before the First World War the average market production of grain of large landed estates in Russia comprised 47 per cent of their total output, that of large peasant holdings 34 per cent, and that of small peasant holdings, only 11.2 per cent.[10]

The liquidation of large landed estates and large-scale peasant farms, which had supplied the market with over 35 per cent of all marketed grain, and the continuous subdivision of peasant holdings were not alone responsible for lowered market production. The Soviet government persistently strove to appropriate agricultural products through compulsory requisitioning, high taxes, or the creation of price disparities between agricultural and industrial goods (the so-called 'scissors'). This policy served to deprive the peasants of all incentives to expand market production.

The agrarian revolution of 1917 abolished the privileges of the nobility and the church and gave legal equality to the peasants. But it did not succeed in solving the problem of poor harvests and chronic crop failures. Nor was it able to solve the problem of supplying urban food needs. New radical agrarian reform was imperative if the level of agricultural productivity was to be raised sufficiently to improve the standard of living of both city and village. This could be done only if Russia were to abandon primitive forms of agriculture for modern methods. The antiquated three-field system had to give way to modern crop rotation, the wooden plow and flail to the metal plow and threshing machine, extensive methods to intensive methods. On the other hand, there was required a government policy that would encourage broad economic development in agriculture.

The policy of zigzags and half-hearted concessions pursued by

[9] Kondrat'yev, op. cit. pp. 211-23.
[10] *Pravda*, 2 June 1928.

the government during the NEP period affected the economy adversely. It failed to stimulate the development of agriculture sufficiently or to supply the city adequately with the necessary material resources. Developments in the NEP period tended in the direction of solving the agrarian problem by the creation of a limited class of rich and powerful peasants at the expense of the rest of the village. But the Soviet government, ideologically and politically opposed to the creation of a rich peasantry, would not consistently encourage the development of individual farm ownership.

It long vacillated between granting partial privileges to encourage rural development, and such policies as struggling against 'rent abuses and hired labor in the village,' and kulaks, i.e. peasants who owned two or three horses. In 1929, the government decided to industrialize the nation and adopted the first Five Year Plan. This program demanded tremendous investments of capital, which, under Russian conditions, could be obtained only from the villages and only on condition of their rapid economic development. It was imperative to choose a definite economic policy. The encouragement of a 'strong peasantry' implied a corresponding distribution of national income and, consequently, a much slower rate of industrialization than that projected by the authors of the Five Year Plan. It would also confine the Revolution to agrarian reforms and political democratization, while considerably restricting in scope the socializing measures of the government.

In the same year, after some hesitation and internal Party struggle, crowned by a surprising declaration of Stalin, which, in fact, contradicted the Five Year Plan, the victorious faction adopted complete socialization. It was decided to organize agriculture along the lines of highly productive, large-scale collective farming, as well as to establish *sovkhozes* (government farms), and to abolish individual peasant farming within the shortest possible time. The first Five Year Plan called for the collectivization of only 18 per cent of all land under cultivation. There began, however, particularly after Stalin's pronouncement 'on transition to the policy of liquidating the kulaks as a class' and the subsequent decision of the Central Committee of the Communist Party 'to carry out full collectivization,' such a rapid process of compulsory collectivization that, by the end of the Five Year Plan, more than two-thirds of all land under cultivation had been collectivized.[11]

Both in organizational methods and tempo, compulsory collectivization begun in 1929 was completely unlike the collectivization of the first Soviet years. The new policy, both painful and ruthless, aroused stubborn resistance on the part of broad sections of the peasantry and was carried out at the cost of millions of peasant lives and the destruction of vast national wealth. The government accomplished the task by ruthless coercion. Relying on the poorest strata of the village, the landless, the horseless, the chronically starved; utilizing their hatred of the village 'rich' and their longing for a better life; applying all forms of administrative and economic pressure—it succeeded, in the course of several years, in liquidating individual peasant farming and making the kolkhoz the dominant economic form.

In 1929, 3.9 per cent of former individual peasant farms and 4.9 per cent of cultivated land area were collectivized. By 1931, 52.7 per cent of peasant farms and 67.8 per cent of cultivated area were collectivized. By 1935 the kolkhozes embraced 83.2 per cent of all farms and 94.1 per cent of all cultivated land. In 1940 they embraced 96.9 per cent of all farms and 99.9 of all cultivated land.[12] It may be said that, on the outbreak of the Russo-German war in 1941, collectivization of agriculture had been fully accomplished.

[11] Gosplan, *Five Year Plan for the Development of the National Economy* (Moscow, 1929); Stalin's speech to the conference of agrarian Marxists, 27 December 1929, in *Pravda*, 29 December 1929; decision of the Central Committee of the Communist Party, 5 January 1930; decree of 1 February 1930.

[12] Central Statistical Office, *Socialist Construction in the U.S.S.R.* (Moscow, 1936), p. 85. *Problems of the Economy* (1941), No. 1, p. 34.

When it embarked on the policy of mass collectivization, the Soviet government decided to promote the artel as the collective form best suited to the economic and cultural level of the country and to Soviet policy. The process of converting communes and tozes into artels was rapid. In 1929 tozes comprised 60.2 per cent of all collectives, communes 6.2, and artels 33.6 per cent; by 1934 communes comprised but 1.8, tozes 1.9, and artels 96.3 per cent of all functioning kolkhozes.

The government aimed not only to raise agricultural productivity, but also to strengthen its own rural economic position. From their inception, kolkhozes required government assistance, both in financing and in obtaining machinery. Government aid was given in the form of loans, seed, and machines. In 1930, a new policy was adopted. Instead of distributing tractors, threshers, and other machines directly to kolkhozes, the government set up Machine-Tractor Stations to service the kolkhozes. At first these were organs of the kolkhozes. In 1931, they became joint enterprises of the kolkhozes and the government. In 1932 they were transformed into purely government organs, servicing collective farms with tractors and combines at fixed fees. When the government decreed that all large machines servicing kolkhozes be concentrated in Machine-Tractor Stations, it became the owner of all the instruments of production, rural as well as urban. In the rural areas it now owned both the land and all large machines. The kolkhozes were thus placed in a position of even greater economic dependence on the government.[13]

In 1930 there were 158 Machine-Tractor Stations in the U.S.S.R., servicing 27.4 per cent of all kolkhozes. In 1940 there were 6,980 stations, servicing 94.5 per cent of all kolkhozes.

Kolkhoz land belongs to the government and cannot be alienated by the kolkhozes or their members. It is attached to the kolkhoz for permanent use. Work animals are kolkhoz property. Cattle and poultry belong in part to the kolkhoz, in part to indi-

[13] Economic Institute of the Academy of Sciences, *The Development of Soviet Economy* (Moscow, 1940), p. 384.

vidual members, within limits set by law. Productive machinery, with the exception of small tools, belongs, as already mentioned, to the government, which, by agreement, works the land and harvests for the kolkhozes. Labor is furnished by the kolkhoz, which, in addition, is obliged to assign a specified percentage of its manpower to certain compulsory tasks (road work, transportation, felling timber, etc.) and to work in urban factories.[14]

The product is divided between the kolkhoz, its individual members, and the government. The last-named takes its share in various forms. In addition to compulsory deductions in money and kind, there are fees for the services of Machine-Tractor Stations, and direct and indirect taxes. The kolkhoz receives its share in the form of allocations to compulsory funds and reserves. The individual kolkhoz member receives his share[15] as compensation for labor; the amount of compensation depends on the size and profitableness of the kolkhoz as a whole.

In addition to collective work, there is a field of enterprise in kolkhozes in which private-property factors have a broad opportunity for development. Each household is granted a plot of land for individual cultivation. Generally these small homesteads are cultivated intensively, and all income from their output belongs to their holders. These homesteads do far more than provide for the fuller satisfaction of peasant consumer needs. Within a short time they have become an important part of the national economy, supplying a good deal of the meat and dairy products, vegetables, fruit, poultry, honey, and eggs.

During the first years of compulsory collectivization, kolkhozes varied greatly in size. The majority consisted of five or six households, cultivating fifteen to twenty hectares. There were also giant kolkhozes of thousands of households, with tracts of cultivated land up to 2,000 or 3,000 hectares in area. The size of the kolkhoz depended largely on the speed of and forms assumed by compulsory collectivization in the particular region.

[14] See Chapter III.b.
[15] See Chapter XV.

It soon became clear that small kolkhozes were not profitable and that giant kolkhozes did not lend themselves to efficient management. By 1938 the average kolkhoz comprised 78 households and 484 hectares of land under collective cultivation. Size varies with region, depending on crops and specialization. Ukrainian kolkhozes, producing mainly grain or cattle, are the largest. In 1935, 65.2 per cent of all Ukrainian kolkhozes covered more than 500 hectares; and 1.1 per cent, less than 100 hectares each. The smallest kolkhozes were found in Georgia (grapes, medicinal herbs, tea), where 65.8 per cent of all kolkhozes covered less than 100 hectares, and only 1.8 per cent more than 500 hectares.[16]

In recent years, kolkhozes have been the chief form of agricultural enterprise in the U.S.S.R. According to data for 1937, they produced 62.9 per cent of total agricultural output, State farms 9.3 per cent, homestead plots 21.5 per cent, workers' suburban plots 4.8 per cent, and individual independent peasants 1.5 per cent. In 1938, kolkhozes produced 86 per cent of all the grain, 30-35 per cent of all the livestock and animal products, and 90-95 per cent of all cotton, sugar beet, flax, and oil-yielding crops.[17]

Despite ruthless and coercive methods of collectivization, which aroused much bitterness against the kolkhozes, reorganization of the entire agricultural economy along the lines of large mechanized enterprises using advanced methods has begun to yield positive results. The agricultural output is rising, land productivity has improved, livestock breeding has begun to recover, rural production for the market has risen, and extreme fluctuations of crop yield, formerly habitual in Russian agriculture, have considerably abated. The average annual grain crops in millions of tons were

[16] T. Basyuk, *The Organization of Socialist Agriculture* (Moscow, 1939), p. 27.

[17] Central Statistical Office, *Socialist Agriculture of the U.S.S.R.* (Moscow, 1939), p. 87; Gosplan, *Agricultural Economy* (Moscow, 1939), p. 214. All figures are in metric tons and refer to the territory of Soviet Russia as of 1938.

67.6 in 1910-14; 73.6 in 1928-32; 94.5 in 1933-7; 95 in 1938; 110.3 in 1939; and 119 in 1940.[18]

The kolkhoz has been economically consolidated; it is the new and predominating form of the life and work of the Soviet peasantry, the overwhelming mass of the population of the U.S.S.R.[19]

[18] Ministry of Agriculture, 'Report of the Ministry of Agriculture,' in *Statistical-Economic Data on Russian Agriculture* (Petersburg, 1916); *Bulletin of Soviet Russian Economics*, edited by S. N. Prokopovich (Prague, April 1934; Geneva, December 1940); *Socialist Agriculture of the U.S.S.R.* (cited above), p. 61; Report of Voznesenski, Chief of the Gosplan, in *Pravda*, 19 February 1941. There are many reasons for believing these official figures on crop yield to be exaggerated. Prokopovich says they should be cut by 10 per cent beginning with 1933. But no reasonable corrective coefficient can alter the conclusion that, in comparison with 1910-14, the crop level has risen and that grain yields tend to rise steadily.

[19] Of the policy of German authorities toward kolkhozes in occupied Russia, little is known. The scanty reports are in part inconsistent. A few facts can, nevertheless, be established with some certitude. Collectivization contradicts the principles of National-Socialist land policy. In fact, however, Hitler's promise to abolish it was only partly fulfilled. In the territory incorporated into the Soviet Union shortly before the Russo-German war (Latvia, Lithuania, Estonia, Eastern Galicia), the kolkhoz had not taken root when German forces occupied those lands. Here the Germans themselves generally undertook the administration of former private farms and estates, or returned them to their former private owners. But in the old Soviet territory (the Ukraine) private agricultural property was not restored. While a decree 'On the new order in agriculture' issued 27 February 1942 by Alfred Rosenberg, Reich Minister for the Ostland, proclaimed the complete abolition of collectivization, it introduced 'agricultural associations' embracing the territories of the respective kolkhozes. Each association was headed by a manager, appointed by German authorities. All able-bodied members of an association participated in plowing, sowing, and harvesting. Household plots became the private property of the individual peasants. Sovkhozes and Machine-Tractor Stations were run by German authorities.

The German press occasionally tried to explain the policy. 'To apply rigidly the principle of kolkhoz liquidation would mean a complete decline of agricultural production' (*Ostdeutscher Beobachter*, 28 February 1942). 'Elastic measures of transition are necessary' (*Koelnische Zeitung*, 3 March 1942). 'The new regulatory measures aim at conserving the capacity of Russian agriculture to produce surpluses for the population as well as for our soldiers and, in the future, for Germany and the whole continent of Europe' (*Pariser Zeitung*, 9 March 1942).

German economic policy—on the whole one of looting—warrants no permanent social or economic conclusion. There can be no doubt, however, that to maintain production the occupying forces had to abstain from dismembering the kolkhoz fields or abolishing collective cultivation and harvesting. The liquidation of the kolkhozes proved a difficult problem.

In the great Russian offensive of 1943, the Red army retook a large part of the territory formerly occupied by the Germans, and on 21 August the Council of People's Commissars and the Central Committee of the Communist Party passed a decree 'On immediate measures to rehabilitate economic life in the regions freed from German occupation' (*Izvestiya*, 22 August 1943). The main aim of the decree is to effect a speedy and planned recovery of the kolkhozes. For this purpose the State organizes the return of evacuated livestock and agricultural implements, extends large credits to the kolkhozes, alleviates taxes, etc. On this decree see *Economist* (London), 25 September 1943.

XI

Constitution and Administration

TO organize kolkhozes and to determine efficient methods of administration were difficult tasks. Socially and economically, kolkhozes were so new a form that it was impossible to organize them on the basis of experience in the administration of industrial enterprises, of large estates in Russia, or of large-scale farms in the United States. New forms of organization and administration had to be sought empirically. There were groping and serious blunders. Forms developed in the course of several years of practical work.

The first kolkhozes (1917-28) arose out of the wishes of peasants or on the initiative of local Communist organizations. They functioned either without fixed rules or with rules that, having been developed in the course of work, differed greatly from one kolkhoz to another, particularly in regard to the interrelation of co-operative and individual factors. In 1930, at the height of the effort toward 'full compulsory collectivization' and the drive against kulaks, the central organs of government developed the first set of statutes for kolkhozes.[1] These did not attempt to regulate internal life, but consisted of instructions on organization; a definition of eligibility for membership; a definition of kulaks (subject to confiscation); a definition of property of members subject to collectivization; and regulations of relations between kolkhozes and government organizations.

These somewhat incomplete statutes, which served neither to regulate administration nor to protect members' interests, re-

[1] Decree of 1 March 1930.

mained in force until 1932. Then, after a period of sharp compulsory collectivization, a series of new decrees [2] was issued, substantially altering the internal administration of kolkhozes and reducing the arbitrary element in relations between kolkhozes and government.

These decrees were dictated by a desire to consider the mood of the peasants and to strengthen their economic interest in improving kolkhoz work. They legalized the right of kolkhoz members to carry on homestead farming, in addition to participating in the work of the kolkhoz. They abolished collectivization of cows and poultry, permitted kolkhozes to sell 'surplus output' on the market, and established quotas for the compulsory delivery of produce to the government. At the same time, these decrees strengthened political control over the managerial personnel of the kolkhozes, and reduced interference by local Party and State organizations.

In 1935, after the economic consolidation of the collective system, a 'Model Statute for Artels,' proposed by Stalin at the Second Congress of kolkhoz shock brigaders, was adopted and subsequently ratified by the highest Party and government organs.[3] With slight modifications, this is the statute under which kolkhozes operate today.

Changes and fluctuations in government policy toward kolkhozes (the drive against kulaks, the struggle against fictitious collectivization, distrust of the wealthier and reliance on the poorest rural elements, the rule of 'appointees,' direction by political bodies, training of leaders, etc.) have all affected kolkhoz forms and methods of administration. Having survived all these fluctuations, the kolkhozes have, since 1935, begun to function under relatively stable conditions, without sharp changes in organizational structure. Revolutionary conditions of compulsory col-

[2] Decree of 4 February 1932, 'On current legislative enactments for the organizational-economic consolidation of kolkhozes'; decree of 10 May 1932; decree of 25 June 1932, 'On revolutionary law.'

[3] Decree of 17 February 1935.

lectivization have been left behind, giving way to a period of evolution and internal consolidation.

The Model Statute of 1935 defines the legal status of the kolkhoz, the forms of its administration and organization, and its relation to other organizations. It is the 'supreme basic law, stabilizing agricultural production in the U.S.S.R.' [4] In a special decree, the Central Committee of the Communist Party and the Council of People's Commissars instructed Party organs that 'the Statute shall not only formally but in reality have the force of a basic State law. Violations must be severely punished.' [5] And, in fact, the Statute plays a supremely important role in the life of the kolkhoz, regulating all its activities and defining all its rights and obligations.

Its definition of the kolkhoz as an independent, voluntary association of peasants is, however, entirely false. While the Statute provides that the kolkhoz be built on the basis of voluntary membership, the overwhelming majority of kolkhozes were organized through coercion. The government resorted to a variety of methods to achieve full collectivization, but administrative and economic pressures were decisive. The usual method of organizing kolkhozes was as follows:

On the initiative of Communists, the poorer elements of a village adopted a resolution to organize a kolkhoz. The property of the well-to-do was then confiscated and turned over to the kolkhoz. Peasants who actively resisted were arrested and sent into forced labor. Those who, in various ways, tried to avoid joining were deprived of the possibility of buying industrial commodities and were subjected to special taxes. Peasants who joined the kolkhozes received tax exemptions and special privileges in marketing 'surpluses' and purchasing manufactured goods. In the light of these circumstances, kolkhozes can hardly be considered voluntary organizations.

Their operation is also subject to the strictest government con-

[4] *Bolshevik* (1938), No. 10-11, p. 18.
[5] Decree of 19 December 1935.

trol and supervision. The government has not only imposed binding regulations but it also directs, through periodic orders, their plans and operations, and maintains rigid control over their entire administrative apparatus.

The Statute of 1935, which is still in force, decrees the collectivization of all work animals, agricultural machinery, seed stocks, feed for collectivized livestock, and farm buildings needed by the collective. Dwellings, some cattle and poultry, and homestead farm buildings remain in the private ownership of individual kolkhoz households; smaller farm tools needed on the homestead farm are not collectivized. Under certain conditions, a kolkhoz can expropriate a member's homestead farm.

The land belongs to the State, but it is attached to the kolkhoz for permanent joint cultivation. Each member is granted a plot ranging from one-quarter to one-half a hectare in area for homestead and private use in gardening, small-animal and poultry breeding, bee-keeping and dairying. Each household may own a cow, one or two calves of horned cattle, pigs, up to ten sheep and goats, twenty hives, and an unlimited number of poultry and rabbits. In some regions variations are permitted in the area of the homestead farm (up to one hectare) and in the number of privately owned livestock.

The kolkhoz consists of peasants of both sexes, over sixteen years of age, who personally participate in its work. On joining the kolkhoz, each peasant must surrender his large farm implements, stock of seed, and work animals. If he has sold his horses during a period of two years prior to joining, and possesses no seed, he must pledge himself to pay in installments, out of future income, the value of a horse and the required seed. The size of the admission share does not affect the member's income.

A member's existence as an individual farmer is at an end. According to the Statute, he may leave the kolkhoz. In such cases his money share may be refunded and he may be compensated by the People's Commissariat for Agriculture 'out of land reserves only, and without damaging the kolkhozes by land fragmentation.' This means, in fact, that any member who leaves loses his entire land share (including the household plot) and the possibility of farming.

The kolkhoz is now governed by the following bodies or persons: the general membership meeting, the Managing Board, the Chairman, the Control Commission, brigade and squad leaders, managers of livestock farms and other auxiliary enterprises, bookkeepers, and various specialists.

The Statute of 1935 proclaims that the administration of kolkhozes be on the principle of self-government. It defines the general membership meeting as the highest organ of kolkhoz administration. The meeting must be held not less than twice monthly. It elects the Managing Board and Control Commission, ratifies production plans, budget, building plans, instructions to brigade leaders, output quotas, estimates of work days, contracts with the Machine-Tractor Station, allocations to various funds, and internal rules. The general membership meeting also has the power of expulsion of members.

The Managing Board is the kolkhoz executive organ. It is elected by the general membership meeting for two years and consists of from five to nine members, depending on the size of the kolkhoz. The kolkhoz Chairman, elected by the general membership meeting for a term of two years, functions as Chairman of the Managing Board. The latter elects from among its members one or two vice-chairmen. The management is responsible for the accounting of output, labor, and money, according to the rules determined by the local and central organs of the People's Commissariat for Agriculture. The Board assigns to its members various functions of management in the economy and productive work of the kolkhoz. According to the Statute, the Managing Board allocates credits within the limits of the budget ratified by the general membership. The Chairman directs all current work; under the law, he can be removed from his post before the expiration of his term only by a court decree or by decision of the general membership meeting. The Control Commission, consisting of three to five persons, is elected for two years. It audits cash and accounts quarterly and checks on the efficiency and legality of all work of the kolkhoz and its organs. The accountant may be selected by the Managing Board from among the kolkhoz members, or may be hired. Within the limits of the budget, the accountant manages the funds of the kolkhoz, makes deductions for stock reserves, records work days of and advances to members, keeps accounts, statistical records, etc. All expense vouchers must be countersigned by the Chairman or a vice-chairman, and by the accountant.

Thus, the Statute fairly consistently sustains the principle of kolkhoz self-government. It would be incorrect to say that the Statute is entirely disregarded. It is followed rigidly in everything relating to the duties of both the kolkhoz and its members. It closely regulates internal administrative and economic activities. But it is far from the reality of kolkhoz relations with the government. Here the kolkhoz functions along entirely different lines, far removed from the spirit and the principles of the Statute. Here self-government and the right of the general membership meeting to decide basic questions are, to a great extent, quite fictitious. All decisions on important questions are previously determined by State and Party organs. All important matters, such as deductions from kolkhoz funds, decentralization of labor, methods of compensation for work, etc., are decided by organs of the central government without preliminary discussion in the kolkhozes. The general membership meeting is obliged to accept government decisions on all important questions. In the discussion of local and current questions, general membership meetings have a somewhat greater function, but even here the outcome is pre-determined by decisions of the Communist group in the kolkhoz. Only in recent years has the Party group been forced to consider majority opinion to some extent.

The question of self-government in the kolkhoz is decisive. That real conditions fail to conform to the Statute and lack the co-operative elements which Lenin believed would stimulate membership activity are facts which have frequently troubled political leaders. In public speeches (26 March and 25 June 1932; 15 February 1935) Stalin has spoken of the necessity of 'leaving all decisions to the kolkhozes themselves,' 'not to substitute administrative bullying and bossing for guidance,' 'not to impose decisions on the kolkhozes,' etc. But the need to obtain from the kolkhozes foodstuffs for cities and raw materials for factories, the hostility of a considerable part of the collectivized peasantry to government policies (a result of compulsory collectivization), and the early economic weakness of the kolkhozes created a situation in which the very speeches of Stalin and government decrees violated the principle of self-government and prompted local State organs to encroach upon it further, imposing their decisions on the kolkhozes.

In recent years, following the economic consolidation of the kolkhozes, the influence of members' opinions has slowly begun to increase. Self-government has begun to be realized in practice, although still in very incomplete forms.

Compared to the constant struggle between the kolkhoz and the government, relations among the various organs within the kolkhoz are relatively unimportant. The struggle over 'one-man control,' important in the early days of Soviet factories, assumed no sharp character in the kolkhozes. It manifested itself in the struggle for leadership between the general membership meeting and the Chairman or, more often, between the Managing Board and the Chairman. In view of the co-operative theory of the kolkhoz, there could be no dispute in principle regarding the decisive role of the general membership meeting. According to the Statute, the Chairman must carry out both the law and the decisions of the meeting. In practice, however, he directs all work, merely reporting to the Managing Board and the general membership meeting. Friction between the Chairman and the Managing Board over jurisdiction is common. In these conflicts the Chairman usually has the support of government and Party organs.

The Chairman is, in fact, responsible both to government organs and to the members of the collective. He must do much to organize smooth and successful functioning. He must fulfil all government demands with respect to the compulsory delivery of goods, labor duties, 'curbing individualistic tendencies,' etc. He is the first to bear the brunt of dissatisfactions of the mass of peasant members. He is held responsible for grievances and unsatisfactory results. If he yields to the pressure of the peasants among whom he must live and work, he is subject to disciplinary action by the government. If he unquestioningly fulfils all the demands of the District Soviet and of local organs of the People's Commissariat for Agriculture, regardless of the mood of the peasant mass, he provokes sharp resentment among the members and often finds himself in a situation in which productive work is utterly impossible. The Chairman must maneuver more or less successfully between the demands of the government and the needs of the kolkhoz members, in extreme cases indicating to the government the necessity of yielding to urgent peasant demands. Chairmanship is thus an extremely difficult and responsible task. It was not by accident that, in the first period of collectivization, the Chairman, when not a city worker sent by the government, or a local friend of the Party, was sometimes chosen by lot from among the kolkhoz members.

In recent years, as the kolkhozes have become economically stronger and as their relations with the government have been relatively stabilized on the basis of definite if exacting law, kolkhozes have begun to produce personalities capable of leadership. At the same time, the functions of the Chairman have become considerably easier and have begun to resemble the usual ones of a manager of an economic enterprise.

XII

Organization of Work

THE most important and complex problem of kolkhoz management is the organization of work. This reflects all the social and economic peculiarities of the kolkhoz form of agriculture. The tendency of development has been away from an initial centralization toward increasing decentralization. At the outset, 'full collectivization' prevailed and, until about 1931, the policy was to centralize administration of land cultivation, animal husbandry, etc., in the hands of the kolkhoz Chairman. All work was conducted under his direction, and workers were transferred from one task to another as work might require. Individuals were attached to no specific task. Work animals and implements went from hand to hand as assignments changed. This system was attributed to the weakness of the administrative apparatus, to government distrust of the majority of kolkhoz members, and to the shortage of capable personnel.

The tendency toward centralization was, moreover, an effort to counteract attempts of peasants to preserve in disguised forms remnants of individual farming. In many kolkhozes, collective fields were divided into small plots and entrusted to groups of members for cultivation. Thus peasant families contrived to hold and work their old land. Similarly, collectivized implements and animals were assigned to groups composed of their former owners. Sometimes there were also concealed forms of land rental, hiring of labor, fictitious work-day records, etc. In its struggle against such deviations, the government tried centralizing the direction of work in the hands of Managing Boards, who could be easily checked on.

It soon became clear, however, that the centralized method of organizing work produced negative results. Management was superficial, workers were constantly shifted from task to task, no individual or group was responsible for a definite cycle of work (e.g. plowing, sowing, harvesting), work became impersonal, and it was impossible to encourage conscientious and efficient performance.

In 1931 many kolkhozes began dividing their membership into brigades for land cultivation, animal husbandry, etc. The results were encouraging. The decree of 4 February 1932 ordered decentralization of management, thus formally recognizing the brigade system. 'Instead of working in a crowd, kolkhozes were broken into smaller brigades of permanent composition and with definite tasks.'[1] The brigade principle was taken over in the Statute of 1935.

Today the brigade is the basic unit in the kolkhoz system. Selection of members is by brigade leaders appointed by the Managing Board and subject to its approval. The composition of a brigade is fixed for the period of its task, usually the duration of the agricultural cycle (i.e. a crop year, the period required for breeding stock, and the like). The average brigade consists of thirty to sixty persons, depending on the crop and specialization. Brigades are further subdivided into squads. Brigades and squads are assigned to definite tasks, usually consisting of related agricultural processes, such as plowing, sowing and harvesting a given sector, increasing a herd of cows by 30 per cent, preparing several thousand tiles. The brigade is assigned a specified tract of farm land, a group of work animals and tools, or a herd, tract of meadow, and fodder. Brigades and squads are responsible for property entrusted to them and the quality of work performed. The Managing Board assigns brigade tasks annually. Stock-breeding, raising poultry or rabbits, and other auxiliary enterprises (flour mills, drying plants, brickyards, etc.), are also

[1] Yakovlev, director of the agricultural department of the Central Committee of the Communist Party, in *Izvestiya*, 5 February 1932.

carried out by brigades and squads. The managers of such enterprises may be appointed from among kolkhoz members or may be hired specialists.

The role of the brigade leader is extremely responsible. He selects the staff of the brigade and manages its sector of the economy. He allocates work within the brigade, maintains discipline, is responsible for quality of performance, keeps the record of work days and other primary data needed for cost accounting. He is responsible to the kolkhoz Chairman for results. 'The new structure of the kolkhoz provides for direct contact between the kolkhoz Chairman, who daily supervises the entire kolkhoz economy, and the brigade leader.' [2] Brigade leaders, according to law, are appointed by the Managing Board for a term of two to three years. A leader may be removed only with the approval of the local organ of the People's Commissariat for Agriculture or the Machine-Tractor Station.

There has been a long struggle against attempts of kolkhoz members to evade work in the kolkhoz. In 1932 and 1933 over 50 per cent of the members did less than 30 days of kolkhoz work annually. The Second Congress of kolkhoz shock brigaders (1935) decreed, as a condition of membership, that each able-bodied person show a minimum record of 50 work days annually. In 1939 the minimum was raised to 60, 80 and 100 work days, depending on the region and the basic specialization of the kolkhoz.[3] A 1937 study showed that, on the average, kolkhoz members worked for the kolkhoz 46.6 per cent of their working-time. The rest was spent on private holdings, in crafts, markets, transportation, etc. During recent years the number of working days per kolkhoz member has increased.[4]

Kolkhozes are obligated to supply workers to factories, State

[2] T. Basyuk, *The Organization of Socialist Agriculture* (Moscow, 1939), p. 83.

[3] Decree of 27 May 1939.

[4] Central Statistical Office, *The Kolkhozes in the Second Five Year Plan* (Moscow, 1939), p. 56. On compensation of kolkhoz members, see Chapter xv, below.

farms (sovkhozes), building operations, road construction and maintenance, etc. Peasants doing seasonal work away from home under the orders or with the permission of the kolkhoz do not thereby lose membership rights.

All work in kolkhozes is, as a rule, performed by members. Specialists, such as agronomists, cattle breeders, veterinarians, technicians, and mechanics, may be legally, and usually are, hired from outside. Until recently, individual non-member peasants were often hired by kolkhozes at harvest time; this practice was always illegal.

XIII

Relation to Government and Other Organizations

FROM the start, all kolkhoz work has been conducted under the constant direction and control of government and Party agencies. The question of the 'triangle'—managers, Party, trade union—so acute in the early administration of State factories, assumed a somewhat different character in agriculture. Rural trade unions had always been weak and never claimed a share in the administration of the kolkhozes. Here the triangle was composed of representatives of the government, the Communist Party, and the kolkhoz.

Government organs with which the kolkhoz must deal are the District Soviet Executive Committee (*Raiispolkom*), the local (village) Soviet, agencies of the People's Commissariat for Agriculture, Machine-Tractor Stations. The highest government agency in a district, the District Soviet Executive Committee, generally directs the entire work of the district's kolkhozes. Such direction has never weakened, although it has changed in form with changes in government policies. In 1929-32 the chief task of the District Executive Committee was the accomplishment of compulsory collectivization and the liquidation of the kulaks. Later it was to organize kolkhoz functioning, to select and train qualified kolkhoz administrators, and to enforce obligations imposed on the kolkhozes by the government. The District Soviet Executive Committee still retains general supervision over the work of kolkhozes. It gives orders regarding policy towards individual peasants applying for membership, fixes quotas for grain collection, ratifies production plans, resolves conflicts between kolkhozes and other local organizations. Generally it enforces policies through the local Soviets, but in such important matters as non-fulfilment of grain collections, violations of sowing plans, epidemics, sharp conflicts, it sends special agents to the kolkhozes.

Direction of current production work is carried out by regional and district offices of the People's Commissariat for Agriculture and by the Machine-Tractor Stations. The former decide questions of general agrarian policy and those affecting kolkhoz cadres. Distinction must be made here between kolkhozes serviced by Machine-Tractor Stations and those that are not; the latter are directed by Commissariat organs. On the other hand, the work of kolkhozes serviced by Machine-Tractor Stations, comprising the vast majority, is directed by the Stations in so far as land cultivation is concerned, and by the Commissariat with respect to other branches (animal husbandry, gardening, bee-keeping, etc.).[1] The role of the Machine-Tractor Stations in the operation of kolkhozes is generally great. Besides their functions in tilling, sowing, and harvesting, they directly supervise all current work of the kolkhozes. Between 1933 and 1935, when every Machine-Tractor Station had its Political Department, the latter was the immediate authority on questions of current operation and carried out its decisions through general membership meetings or orders to Chairmen. The Machine-Tractor Stations were thus the 'chief lever in the reorganization of agriculture along socialist principles.'[2] Since 1935 kolkhoz operations have been freed of direct interference by the Machine-Tractor Stations, but the latter still supervise. 'They help the kolkhozes set up plans of production and finance. They fix the correct crop-rotation system, assist in the organization of work and the allocation of income, the training of leaders, the setting up of accounting systems, the organiza-

[1] Decree of 4 April 1934.

[2] Kaganovich, Report to the Central Committee and the Central Executive Committee of the Communist Party, 23 January 1933.

tion of competition, and the struggle to increase soil productivity.'[3]

Economic relations between Stations and kolkhozes are fixed by contracts based on a model approved by the Council of People's Commissars on 17 February 1934. Such contracts must be ratified by the general meeting of the kolkhoz.

The organs of the Communist Party play no less a role in the life of the kolkhoz. They direct every important step in its activities. Between 1929 and 1935 a hidden but stubborn struggle went on between Party and government organs for control of kolkhoz productive activity. Characteristically, the Party organs fought not so much against the District Soviet Executive Committees or the Machine-Tractor Stations, whose chiefs were always Communists, as against the local organs of the Commissariat for Agriculture, where the decisive role was frequently played by agricultural specialists. The Statute of 1935 attempted to establish the organs of the Commissariat and the Machine-Tractor Stations as supervisors of productive activity. But the struggle persists. In 1940 *Pravda* wrote that 'Party District Committees have been transformed into a sort of district agricultural office.'[4] A periodical of the Central Committee of the Communist Party also states that 'Party agencies are still striving to displace the organs of the Commissariat for Agriculture.'[5]

Formally, local and district Party organizations have no right to interfere with production, but, as in all other realms of life, they play the determining role in solving major questions, particularly those connected with Party agrarian policies. The Political Departments (composed of Communists) set up in 1933 in each Machine-Tractor Station to direct kolkhoz activities, were important in the first period of kolkhoz organization. Early in 1935 they were abolished and the direction of political work was taken over by the Vice-Chairman of Machine-Tractor Stations

[3] People's Commissariat for Agriculture, *Aid to the Kolkhoz Village* (Moscow, 1939), p. 47.

[4] *Pravda*, 22 March 1940.

[5] *Party Construction* (1941), No. 1, p. 41.

and by special agents of the district and regional Party committees.[6] Despite the strengthening of the regular State organs, the highest Party bodies still consider it necessary to maintain constant and close supervision over kolkhozes. In 1940 the Council of People's Commissars issued a decree placing full responsibility for crop rotation on Party district committees, although this is the function of State agencies, i.e. District Soviet Executive Committees, the Commissariat for Agriculture, and the Machine-Tractor Stations.[7] At the beginning of 1941, almost on the eve of the war, a circular of the Central Committee of the Communist Party instructed Party organizations to 'direct daily the work of enlightenment in the villages, to organize leadership and supervise the execution of instructions of Party and government in the villages.' [8]

Some idea of the enormous number of people in government and Party organs of district and regional centers that are engaged in controlling kolkhoz activities can be gained from the fact that, for the 27,000 kolkhozes of the eastern Ukraine, there were over 29,000 responsible officials in control agencies.[9] Although friction between Party and government organs does not, under Soviet conditions, assume the character of open conflict, the position of the kolkhoz in such an 'interdepartmental struggle' is, nevertheless, quite complicated.

The third member of the 'triangle,' the kolkhoz itself, was at first a helpless object. 'The kolkhoz peasant is completely removed from control in the organization of production.' [10] 'He must play merely the passive role of a labor unit.' [11] 'All kolkhoz affairs are decided by the District Executive Committee and the District

[6] Plenum of the Central Committee, November 1934; *Kolkhoz Law*, textbook for law colleges published by the People's Commissariat for Justice (Moscow, 1939), p. 99.

[7] Decree of 18 March 1940.

[8] *Party Construction* (1941), No. 10, p. 4.

[9] *Izvestiya*, 11 February 1941.

[10] *Pravda*, 8 April 1930.

[11] *Izvestiya*, 6 May 1930.

Committee.'[12] The representative of the kolkhoz, its Chairman, could only maneuver between the Party organs and those of the Commissariat for Agriculture, 'registering' the discontent of his members and pleading their needs. Any expression of opposition immediately resulted in removal from the chairmanship by joint action of Party and State organs. True, government decrees and Party orders have frequently and categorically forbidden the appointment or removal of kolkhoz chairmen.[13] In reality, even as late as 1941, there were cited many removals:

In a number of districts there survives the practice of mass removal and transfers of supervisory workers of kolkhozes and Machine-Tractor Stations. In 1940, 78 per cent of chairmen in the Ryazan region were removed and 28 per cent in the Kursk region. In 69 kolkhozes in the Rostov region, 279 chairmen were removed during 1939 and 1940; in kolkhoz 'Sunrise' [*Voskhod*, Rostov region], 22 chairmen were removed in two years.[14]

N. Khrushchov, General Secretary of the Ukrainian Communist Party, in direct contradiction to the Statute of 1935, regards the right of removing and transferring chairmen as belonging exclusively to the *Oblispolkom* (Regional Executive Committee).[15]

Economic power has, however, its own logic. As the economic importance of the kolkhozes grew, as chairmen and Managing Boards ceased to arouse political distrust and gained in skill, the government was obliged, in the interests of production, to refrain from 'direct management,' i.e. interference with current work. Yet, because of the peculiar social structure of the kolkhoz, the emancipation of its elected administration from control by government and Party organs is a far slower process than the comparable one in industrial enterprises. The reality of the process cannot be doubted, however.

[12] *Socialist Agriculture*, 6 May 1937.
[13] *On the Agrarian Front* (1932), No. 1, p. 64.
[14] *Party Construction* (1941), No. 1, p. 37, No. 8, p. 45, No. 10, p. 9.
[15] *Pravda*, 11 February 1941

All questions of taxes, health, and education are decided jointly by the kolkhoz and the local Soviet. In many regions where kolkhozes are economically strong, they have taken over all communal functions of local Soviets: maintenance of roads, lighting, schools, hospitals, etc. At one time, government organs considered abolishing village Soviets and transferring their functions to the kolkhozes, but the central government decided to preserve them as local government branches for maintaining public safety, collecting taxes, issuing legal documents, recording births, marriages, and deaths, etc.

In addition, the kolkhoz has a close relationship with consumer and sales co-operatives, through which it disposes of a part of its production and purchases consumer goods. Where kolkhozes are located near sovkhozes, a constant relationship is maintained. The sovkhoz assists the kolkhoz in procuring selected seeds and blooded stock, while the kolkhoz performs a variety of work for the sovkhoz at harvest time.

XIV

Planning and Accounting

THE kolkhoz system embraces an overwhelming portion of all Soviet agricultural production. Like all Soviet economy, kolkhozes are intended to function within the general national economic Plan. Each kolkhoz has a plan of production, which is a component part of the overall agricultural plan, and thus of the general Plan.

During the first years of 'integral collectivization,' planning was rudimentary. The compulsory nature of collectivization, variations in the size of kolkhozes, fluctuations in membership, the inner social struggle, the 'infantile disease' of the period of organizing, all interfered with planning in the kolkhozes. But as the kolkhozes became stronger, the necessity for planning was dictated by their economic task, social structure, and size. A carefully prepared plan was essential for the rational conduct of large-scale farming embracing hundreds, sometimes thousands, of peasant households, with varying forms of production and a million-rouble annual turnover. It was all the more essential because each kolkhoz, in the midst of current work, faced the task of materially improving its productivity and operating system.

The government has long striven to institute planning in the kolkhozes. In an address to the Plenum of the Central Committee (11 January 1933), Stalin declared: 'The kolkhoz is a large enterprise. But a large enterprise cannot be operated without a plan . . . Without a plan it must perish and disintegrate . . . The plan is the very foundation of the kolkhoz system.'[1] In 1934 a

[1] J. Stalin, *Problems of Leninism* (10th ed., Moscow, 1934), pp. 517-18.

decree [2] ordered agricultural organs, Machine-Tractor Stations, and kolkhozes to operate along planned lines. In connection therewith, the government promulgated a standard plan for kolkhoz production, 'to be followed without deviation.' Similarly, the Model Statute for Artels (1935) contains a provision obligating kolkhozes to operate according to plan.

Thus, both economic and legal factors impel kolkhozes toward planned operation. The formulation of plans involves several stages, of which the most important are (1) the setting of tasks by high State economic authorities; (2) the working out of a draft plan by the kolkhoz; (3) the issuing of a mandatory plan by State authorities.

At the end of each calendar year the District Soviet Executive Committee prepares a one-year 'control program' for the district's economic development. This includes a plan for kolkhozes. Notice, in the form of government assignments ('control figures'), is transmitted to the kolkhozes through Machine-Tractor Stations and organs of the Commissariat for Agriculture. Assignments cover the scope and nature of work projected for each kolkhoz, usually basic specialization (e.g. grain, dairy products, meat) and possible subsidiaries, crop rotation, preparation of cattle-feed, cultivation of new areas, crop yield, level of mechanization (e.g. percentage of mechanization in tilling), limits of expenditures for new construction (in percentages of kolkhoz income), dates for the completion of tasks.

On receipt of its assignment, each kolkhoz, usually through a selected group of members aided by a Machine-Tractor Station, drafts a production plan. The kolkhoz can make no changes in government assignments, even if these contradict previously determined plans of crop rotation or rules of agricultural technique. It 'may submit objections to the District Committee of the Party or the regional agricultural administration.' Assigned tasks do not cover all kolkhoz activities. Selection of crops, extent of sow-

[2] Decree of 4 March 1934.

ing, and internal matters are left to the kolkhoz. Thus, for instance, having received instructions that basic specialization must be in grain, a kolkhoz determines, within the limits of required crop rotation, what grains it will grow and what supplementary crops it will rotate. Until the end of 1939, District Soviet Executive Committees prescribed both the kinds and quantities of crops to be sown, but experience taught the government to allow kolkhozes independence in this. A decree of 28 December 1939 pointed out that 'the existing method of planning grain crops curbs the creative initiative of kolkhoz members and weakens their interest in the struggle for further increase of productivity,' and ordered that 'kolkhozes select crops independently within their assigned plan of sowing and crop rotation.' Kolkhozes must, however, 'absolutely fulfil their obligation to supply the government with specified crops.' [3]

Since 1935, kolkhozes can determine the amount of supplementary crops to be sown. The kolkhoz plans construction work (draining, roads, construction of flour mills, etc.) within prescribed financial limits. It develops plans for secondary and home industries, the organization of work, the supply of legally required products to the government. It drafts a budget, a schedule of assignments to brigades, and a plan for distribution of income to the various kolkhoz funds and to members (in terms of percentages of expected income). It may suggest the introduction of new crops, changes in rotation, the setting up of subsidiary enterprises (e.g. bee-keeping). Such plans must, however, be approved by the district Soviet. Somewhat greater freedom is allowed in the development of plans for the organization of work and for improving quality and quantity of output. But even here, kolkhozes must guide themselves by government orders and circulars of government and Party as well as by the Statute.

The kolkhoz draft plan is transmitted through local, district, and regional administrations to the People's Commissariat for Agri-

[3] Decree of 28 December 1929.

culture. Here it is discussed, amended, fitted into district, regional, and national plans, and finally issued as binding on all lower organs, including the kolkhozes. On receiving the final plan, a kolkhoz determines operating plans, budget, and orders to brigades and managers.

This final production-financial plan embraces all branches of kolkhoz activities and usually consists of plans for the following: (1) sowing; (2) harvesting and threshing; (3) contract with the Machine-Tractor Station; (4) repair and acquisition of agricultural machines and implements; (5) organization of work (division into brigades); (6) increase of crop yield; (7) cultivation of new areas; (8) development of animal husbandry; (9) crafts and home industries; (10) construction; (11) finances (budget, capital investment); (12) fulfilment of obligations to the State; (13) distribution of income; (14) cultural-social activities.

Methods of current accounting and of measuring the success of the work of a kolkhoz and its members are as numerous as in industrial enterprises. The favorite, where applicable, as in sowing, plowing, breeding, repair of tractors, fertilization, is periodic checking (every ten days or every month) of the percentage of plan fulfilment. The results are published in local newspapers as a means of control, of rebuke or encouragement.

As each planned stage of production is completed, it is accounted for in absolute figures. During sowing, progress reports are compiled and published every ten days. As a crop ripens, productivity and probable total yield of each kolkhoz, district, province, and Republic are estimated by sampling. At harvest time, crops gathered and probable total harvest are computed. A similarly careful system is applied in animal husbandry (increase in heads, production of milk, meat, hides, wool, etc.), gardening, and other farming branches. When the productive cycle (usually a year) has been completed, rough and later exact computations are made of yield, productivity, etc. The amount of produce delivered to the government (taxes in kind), the amount sold to the government, the amount sold in the market, the ratio of marketed to total produce, and costs are computed. Finally, net results are reckoned in terms of income in money and kind to the kolkhoz and to members.

'Control by the rouble,'[4] which plays so important a role in industry, is of much less importance in the kolkhozes. Kolkhozes receive little credit from the State Agricultural Bank. Of 181 billion roubles which the third Five Year Plan (1938-42) allocated to all long-term investment, credits and allocations for capital construction in kolkhozes came to but 9.2 billion roubles, i.e. less than 40,000 roubles per kolkhoz.[5] Most kolkhoz purchasing operations are effected without banking aid, since the necessary commodities (e.g. wagons, small implements) are paid for with produce.

According to both law and practice, each level of kolkhoz administration (Chairman, Managing Board, brigade leaders, accountant, Control Commission) reports several times annually to the general membership meeting.

[4] See Chapter VII.
[5] V. Molotov, *The Third Five Year Plan,* Address to the 18th Party Congress (Moscow, 1939), p. 31.

XV

Incomes and Incentives

THIS study is devoted to management. No full and detailed account of the complex problem of compensation of members and allocation of joint product will be attempted. But some attention must be given the subject for two reasons: first, the material incentives for the managerial personnel and those for the rank and file are in many respects similar or interdependent. Second, fair and efficient allocation of income to stimulate the work of individual members, while providing for common funds and for the State, is a major theme of Russian agricultural legislation and naturally affects the tasks of management.

a. Income

The income of both administrative officers and members depends on the quantity and quality of production. Distribution has been successively on a flat basis, on a piecework basis in terms of 'work days,' and on a basis of 'work days' plus bonuses for brigades and squads.

The first kolkhozes distributed income equally to all consumers or workers or in proportion to invested shares. The Statute of 1930 permitted the distribution of 5 per cent of income in proportion to invested shares,[1] but that of 1935 abolished this system as inconsistent with compulsory collectivization and the liquidation of kulaks. A system of equal income distribution to all consumers encouraged able-bodied peasants to register non-productive family members as kolkhoz members and then to go to the

[1] Decree of 13 April 1930.

city to work. A system of distribution of income equally to all workers was somewhat more satisfactory, but also failed to provide an incentive to labor. These two early systems were finally abandoned. Gradually the kolkhozes adopted piecework and computation in terms of 'work days,' a system made compulsory early in 1933.[2]

The Statute fixes compulsory deductions from kolkhoz income to form reserves for seed, fodder, cultural needs, and capital construction. These deductions are made after the discharge of taxation and other obligations to the government. Income remaining after all these payments is divided among members according to work-day credits earned.

A work day is a conventional unit. All work in kolkhozes is divided into seven categories, depending on its nature and complexity. Since the present system is based on piecework, production quotas have been set for each kind of work. Under- or overproduction then affects the number of work-day credits. Thus, the number of work days is determined not only by the category, but also by the quality of work and effort expended. For every day worked, the member is credited with one-half to two work days, depending on the category and quality of performance. One peasant may receive only 12½ work-days credit while another, doing a different job, will receive 50 work-days credit for a full month's work. Members not working receive no credits.

At the end of the year, kolkhoz income and the grand total of days worked are calculated and the 'value' of the work day is determined by dividing income (after statutory deductions) by the total number of work days. Thus the work day of one kolkhoz is not equal in value to that of another, but depends on achievement and thus on the efficiency of the organization of work. To the individual, therefore, the value of the work day (i.e. his compensation unit) is the index of success of kolkhoz work. By making his income directly dependent on total kol-

[2] Decree of 1 March 1933.

khoz income, this system stimulates the individual to efficient work. But it also makes income dependent on efficiency of the organization of work, the performance of other members, loss through unproductive work, accuracy in recording work days, etc.

The shortcomings of this method were officially characterized as follows:

Work in the kolkhozes is estimated one-sidedly. In distributing income, the management of the kolkhoz bases itself only on the number of work days of each member. No account is taken of final results, i.e. what has been raised per hectare,[3] or what has been achieved on a subsidiary farm. The work of individual kolkhoz members, brigades and squads becomes depersonalized, and is not materially encouraged.[4]

Accordingly, a decree issued shortly before the war tried to strengthen the interest of individual kolkhoz officials and members. It ordered:

[the issuing] to members of kolkhoz brigades and squads supplementary compensation in kind, over and above the established compensation in kind, over and above the established compensation for work-day credits, or to make payment in money for a part of the output achieved by the brigade or squad in excess of planned yield of grain, industrial, vegetable, or feed crops, and for over-quota production in animal husbandry.[5]

Under the new regulations, work within planned limits is paid for on the basis of work days. In addition, a specified part of all that a brigade (grain crops) or squad (other produce) produces in excess of quota is turned over to the brigade or squad, or where possible, to the individual instrumental in raising productivity. The bonus is determined at rates higher than the basic rate. In

[3] i.e. by a brigade.

[4] *Bolshevik* (1940), No. 24, pp. 8-20.

[5] Decree 'On Supplementary Compensation for the Work of Kolkhoz Members in Raising the Productivity of Agricultural Crops and the Output of Animal Husbandry,' 31 December 1940.

grain, a brigade receives one-quarter of yield above plan; in flax, one-third; in potatoes and vegetables, one-fifth. In cotton and sugar-beets the bonus has been set at 50 per cent of excess output, but since the government does not permit retention of these products, it is paid in money at the official rate. Dairymaids receive 15 per cent of excess milk; stablemaids (handling cattle) one-half kilogram of meat for every ten kilograms of weight increase per head; hog breeders, every fiftieth suckling pig; poultry maids, 15 per cent of excess eggs and 50 per cent of excess poultry. A similar system has been established for orchards, bee-keeping, rabbit-breeding, etc. Variations in bonus rates reflect both differences in overhead and labor required, and government efforts to encourage particular branches of agriculture.

It is interesting to see how N. Khrushchov, Secretary of the Ukrainian Communist Party, explained the introduction of the new system:

> Thousands and tens of thousands of people in the kolkhozes set an example by model performance. We respect them, we honor them. And now, in addition to honor, they will also receive ten suckling pigs each. That is very good. In addition to honor, they will receive several tons of grain each, or several hundred liters of milk, or several hundred eggs . . . This is both pleasant and useful. And it reaches everyone. Even the 'principled loafer' [6] will now bestir himself . . . Serving his own interest, the kolkhoz member will do better work in the kolkhoz and thus strengthen the kolkhoz economy.[7]

The new decree took into account the feelings of the majority of kolkhoz peasants who had had no interest in improvements, but only in work-day credits ('We'll all be paid the same anyway'). It considerably increased the interest of individual members, squads, and brigades, and especially of the kolkhoz administration in the success of the entire kolkhoz. But it is doubtful

[6] 'Principled loafers,' i.e. loafers out of principle, is a name applied by Soviet Communists to kolkhoz members who explain their insufficient activity by ideological disagreement with kolkhoz methods of work.

[7] *Izvestiya*, 11 February 1941.

whether even this system has created a direct, obvious relation between a member's earnings and the quality and intensity of his labor.

There are two fundamental obstacles to the establishment of such a relation. The first is that every member knows that a large part of income deriving from over-quota production will go for government use or to productive, communal or cultural improvements in the kolkhoz. Even in recent years (1937-9), about 40 per cent of kolkhoz income in kind was taken by the government, about 20 per cent deducted for obligatory funds, and only about 40 per cent distributed among members. Of monetary income, about 55 per cent was distributed to kolkhoz members.

The second obstacle is inherent in kolkhoz administration. The value of the work day is the quotient of the net product available for distribution and the grand total of work days. But since, in all fundamental questions, the kolkhoz is managed by the government and its agencies, neither the individual kolkhoz member, the brigades, nor the general membership meeting can substantially influence either factor.

The new decree regulates the compensation for the work of kolkhoz administrations. The Chairman, in distinction to all other non-hired workers, gets a fixed monthly salary of from 25 to 400 roubles (about 150 roubles average). In addition, he is credited with from 45 to 90 work days monthly, depending on the area under cultivation during the year. Thirdly, when output exceeds plan, he gets a bonus of 15 to 40 per cent of his total salary. Finally, after the first three years, he is credited with 5 to 15 per cent additional bonus for each year of past service. Altogether, he earns 2½ times to 3 times more than the average kolkhoz member. The bonuses make him personally interested in increasing the intensity of labor.

Crop specialists, agronomists, and stockbreeders (usually members of the Managing Board) receive work-day credits and, for over-quota production, 70 per cent of the supplementary compensation paid the Chairman. Brigade leaders and farm managers are credited with one and a half times as many work days as the average kolkhoz member. They also get an over-quota production bonus of one and a half times the average additional compensation of members of their respective brigades. Squad leaders are paid on the level of skilled kolkhoz members, but for over-quota production receive bonuses of 2 to 3 per cent of the value of work days of members of their respective squads. Compensation to accountant and other administrative officials, tractor and combine operators, mechanics and technicians also depends on results of their work or of the kolkhoz as a whole.

In 1932 the State Audit agencies found that such large sums (20-25 per cent of total income) were expended for compensation of administrative and service personnel 'as to constitute pillage of kolkhoz property.'[8] In consequence, it was decreed that no more than 8 per cent of the value of the grand total of work days and no more than 2 per cent of cash income may be used for administrative compensation.[9]

For non-fulfilment of planned crop rotation and production, failure to deliver to the government specified produce, poor accounting, etc., the Chairman, members of the Managing Board, and the accountant are subject to reprimand, fine, arrest, or removal, either administratively or by court decision.

A great stimulus to the efforts of both administration and members is opportunity of promotion to more skilled and better-paid work. A member can be promoted to squad leader, brigade leader, or member of the Managing Board. Chairmen of small kolkhozes can be promoted to larger ones or appointed to posts in district organs of the Commissariat for Agriculture, District Executive Committees, etc. Recently a number of chairmen were nominated and elected to the Supreme Soviet 'in recognition of their excellent work.'

Another strong incentive is the practice of sending, at kolkhoz expense, chairmen, brigade leaders, and tractor operators to insti-

[8] People's Commissariat for Justice, *Kolkhoz Law* (Moscow, 1939), p. 324.
[9] Decree of 10 September 1933.

tutions of higher learning, and members to training courses for brigade leaders, chairmen, tractor operators, and agronomists. Such persons retain membership and are credited with work days according to an established system.

b. Intangible Incentives

Furthermore, there are intangible social and moral incentives. All activity is social and public, carried on in an atmosphere of responsible building of new forms of work and social life. Constant propaganda imbues kolkhoz members with a consciousness of the national importance of their work. They are awake to a desire for a 'new life,' one more secure, freer than that they led under the yoke of large landowners or of which they have heard from their parents. The kolkhoz member is made to realize the necessity of conscientious, efficient labor, or even sacrifice, to build a better future.

In addition, administration and members have been inspired with a sense of competition, a desire to break records. The energy and the desire to excel, which in old rural Russia were expressed in drinking bouts and brawls, are today skillfully directed into competition for productive records. Tractor operators strive to work the largest area in the shortest possible time, crop specialists to achieve a record yield, stock hands to produce more milk and healthier animals. Fiction as well as newspaper reports provide many examples of self-sacrificing, heroic acts of kolkhoz Chairmen and members, performed for purely social motives at critical moments in the life of the kolkhoz—during fires, floods, or crop failures.[10]

A system of honorary orders and titles ('shock-brigader,' 'model worker'), trips to Moscow, display of records at official expositions, publication of portraits in newspapers, demonstra-

[10] I. Sholokhov, *Virgin Soil* (1932), *And Quiet Flows the Don* (4 vols., 1928-40); F. Panferov, *Bruski* (2 vols., 1929, 1930), *With Sure Step* (1934), and *Activity* (1937); U. Usupov, 'The Great Fergana Canal is Completed' in *Pravda*, 21 September 1939.

tions at public meetings, stimulate competition among kolkhozes and their members. The actual general situation of kolkhozes inspires workers with social enthusiasm, a sense of duty, a desire for knowledge, joy of achievement, a striving for records, competitive zeal—one and all.

The kolkhoz youth is particularly active. Raised under revolutionary conditions and educated in the 7-year or 10-year school, young kolkhoz members break easily with the old rural routine, follow eagerly the instructions of the new specialists. It is they who usually create laboratory huts and organize evening courses. With self-sacrificing zeal they initiate competitions for high productivity. They have a keen passion for knowledge, a strong desire for advancement. To earn the title 'Stakhanovite' and, perhaps, a trip to the city or a term in an advanced educational institution, young kolkhoz members are ready to nurse every ear of corn in their brigade's field, every horse on the farm, regardless of time or pay. Studies made in the South (Melitopol district), in Central Russia, the Ukraine, and Kuban, furnish interesting examples of children of kolkhoz families, who, after several years of work in the kolkhoz, completed their education and became doctors, agronomists, engineers, and teachers.[11]

Greater activity among women has also served to improve the quality of work in kolkhozes. The Statute of 1935 devotes a special paragraph to the emancipation of kolkhoz women and prescribes their participation in productive and social activity. About 60 per cent of all shock workers, almost 70 per cent of all squad leaders are women. The kolkhoz wrought basic changes in the position of the peasant woman. She works on equal terms with men, earns her own work-day credits, is economically independent of her husband. These women are usually more conscientious than the men. They seem more enthusiastic in competi-

[11] A. Arina and I. Kotov, *Social-Economic Changes among the Peasantry of the Melitopol District* (Moscow, 1939); I. Laptev, *The Soviet Peasantry* (Moscow, 1939), p. 151.

tion than men, and have achieved record outputs in beets, flax, cotton, milk, and other products. Their cultural and living conditions are still far from those of the peasant woman of Denmark, or the farm wife of Canada, but nurseries, schools, medical aid, and the protection of motherhood make their lives considerably easier than formerly.

XVI

Private vs. *Co-operative Interests*

IN the first years of the regime, Lenin attached great importance to peasant co-operation as 'the best school preparing them for socialist forms of society.' His 'co-operative plan'[1] presupposed

> organization of a powerful socialist industry, capable of fully supplying agriculture with first-class machinery in the form of tractors, combines, electro-motors, etc., thus creating the material basis for an enormous increase in the productivity of agricultural labor and inducing small peasants, by force of example and in their own interest, to change over to large-scale mechanized agriculture.[2]

By organizing peasants in kolkhozes through 'compulsion' rather than 'inducement,' Stalin realized Lenin's co-operative plan in three to five years. All agricultural production became co-operative and the peasantry was transformed into kolkhoz members.

Before the purges and trials, there were heated debates in the Soviet press concerning the social character of kolkhozes. Some Left Communists argued that kolkhozes had fully socialized the rural areas, that they were 'enterprises of consistently socialist character.' 'Right deviators' asserted, on the contrary, that the kolkhozes, like ordinary co-operatives or like the old Russian village communes, merely embodied some common peasant interests, but did not fundamentally affect the principle of private property as a basis of agriculture. There was also, among Com-

[1] 'Plan for the socialist transformation of primitive agricultural production by the gradual involvement of the broadest masses of working peasantry into the stream of socialist construction through co-operation,' in *Collected Works* (Moscow, 1932), XXVII:394-5.

[2] Ibid. XXV:276.

munists, a group that believed that 'the kolkhoz member is a sort of home-industry worker in socialist industry, armed with the latest achievements of agricultural technique, no longer working for the market or for the kulak, but fulfilling orders of socialist industry.' [3] Stalin put an end to these debates by stating that 'the kolkhozes are enterprises of a socialist type. The rest depends upon the content that will fill this form.' [4]

This debate reflected, in distorted and scholastic form, the necessity of determining the true character of present-day kolkhozes. They are, indeed, enterprises of mixed character; as is natural in a revolutionary epoch, they combine different, even contradictory elements of systems of private property and co-operation.

Private property elements are clear. Receipt of income in kind compels individual kolkhoz members to market some produce. The homestead farm, although situated on kolkhoz land and dependent on the kolkhoz for forage, pasturage, transportation, and some other facilities, nevertheless produces directly for the market and yields profit to the individual kolkhoz member. But the absence of private property in the instruments of production, the use of collective methods in the organization of work, the dependence of individual income on the results of effort, both collective and individual, rather than on investment, distinguish the kolkhoz from both individual and corporate private enterprise.

Co-operative elements are common use of land, common work in field, dairy farm, and barn, common ownership of farm buildings and small implements. But the main feature of true producers' co-operation—joint ownership of important instruments of production—is lacking. Tractors, combines, threshing and other complex machines belong to the government and merely service kolkhozes under contract. Tractor and combine operators, mechanics, and chauffeurs, even if kolkhoz members, are hired employees of Machine-Tractor Stations; the kolkhoz merely supplies

[3] *Economic Review* (September 1929), p. 13.
[4] J. Stalin, *Problems of Leninism* (10th ed., Moscow, 1934), p. 287.

the necessary auxiliary and unskilled labor. Other essential co-operative elements that are absent are voluntary participation, economic sovereignty of the membership, and genuine self-government.

Yet these are not mere government enterprises with members as hired labor. Unlike the income of wage earners, that of kolkhoz members depends on the aggregate income of the enterprise. This system also differs substantially from such 'profit-sharing by workers' as is occasionally seen in industrial enterprises where workers are guaranteed a fixed wage regardless of profits or losses.

Nor is it correct to regard kolkhozes as jointly owned by the State and the members, with the State supplying capital and the members furnishing labor.[5] There is joint ownership neither of the enterprise as a whole, nor of the instruments of production, nor of labor. The land belongs to the State, but is at the disposal of the kolkhoz for cultivation. The overwhelming proportion of the productive machinery is outside the kolkhoz and belongs to the State. The labor and some implements belong to the kolkhoz. Each fulfils an economic function but neither merges into a unified economic collective. And the government alone has the power to command.

Thus, the kolkhozes combine features of (a) State enterprises conducted according to Plan and under constant government direction; (b) co-operative enterprises which, although not enjoying self-management, unite and organize members' labor and provide income dependent on labor and on the income of the enterprise as a whole; and (c) small private homesteads working for the market and providing a considerable proportion of their owners' individual incomes.

This combination of elements reflects itself in the psychology and life of the members. The Soviet peasant is not the one who existed for centuries in old Russia. Gone is the former isolation in the struggle against the natural disasters so pervasive of rural life.

[5] L. E. Hubbard, *The Economics of Soviet Agriculture* (New York, 1939), pp. 264, 267, tends to accept this interpretation.

Gone, too, is the helplessness of the impoverished, petty farmers, the economic fatality characteristic of the millions of peasants of China, India, and old Russia.

The peasant does not have economic independence in the kolkhoz. He feels himself to be a component part of a larger economic collective, one gradually proving both its ability to survive and its productive capacity. Recovery from natural disasters is easier and more rapid than of old. While the peasant feels that dependence on the government fetters his initiative, he also sees the government constantly aiding the kolkhoz. The whole process of work is carried on collectively, and common work engenders an awareness of common interests. The conditions surrounding kolkhoz labor to a considerable degree assimilate members' psychology to that of workers in large urban enterprises. Group work, division of labor, collective piecework compensation, planning are all instrumental in furthering this process. More and more, the branches of kolkhoz economy are rebuilt in accordance with industrial methods and forms. There is extensive use of machines, scientific methods of production and processing.

Yet the kolkhoz member is not transformed into a worker whose only means of existence is his labor power. He is co-owner of some small productive implements and owner of his private homestead farm. The receipt of a share of kolkhoz income, the marketing of a share of income in kind—at prices more profitable than those received for sales to the government—keep alive private-property psychology. This effect is strengthened by peasant work on the homestead, a small, but intensively cultivated plot, into which the owner puts his initiative, his desire to possess his own bit of soil, his own cow, his own hives, and from which he receives a relatively high income.

There are two souls in the breast of the kolkhoz peasant, engaged in constant struggle: the soul of the petty proprietor and that of the kolkhoz member. The first draws him to private, the second to collectivized economy. The advantages of the kolkhoz as a large, mechanized economy are daily demonstrated; above all, he knows that since their consolidation there has not been a single disastrous crop failure,[6] that the kolkhoz economy grows from year to year. Thus the peasant evaluates the kolkhoz and stands by it despite bitter grievances, past and present.

The virtual impossibility of resigning from the kolkhoz (nominally the member may do so, but he cannot thereafter get a land allotment [7]) makes it difficult to estimate the degree to which the peasantry has become reconciled to it. Nor are assertions of Soviet writers and journalists altogether reliable in this respect. But, in addition to the fairly convincing evidence of objective conditions —the growing productivity of kolkhozes—there are strong indirect proofs. In the first years of collectivization, peasants were driven into kolkhozes forcibly. Today individual peasants strive to be admitted, while kolkhoz members evince growing reluctance to admit those who want to come in 'when everything has been prepared.' The government is obliged to decree the admission of new members. On the other hand, fewer members volunteer now to do city work. The government must pass laws obligating kolkhozes to send workers to city factories.[8] Formerly, the mass migration of village youth to the cities caused special government measures, to keep them in the kolkhozes. This migration has decreased. In 1940, the government was driven to issue a decree ordering the compulsory mobilization of young kolkhoz members for training in skilled trades.[9]

One hampering feature in the life of the kolkhoz is the lack of opportunity to utilize productively individual savings. Savings of the kolkhoz as a whole may be used for general purposes, productive, social, or cultural. New automobiles are purchased, stables built, brickyards or hulling mills established, gardens planted, road lighting improved, reading-rooms and motion-

[6] It is well known that in pre-Soviet Russia, no decade saw more than three good harvest years or less than two complete crop failures.

[7] See Chapter XI.

[8] B. Babanin, 'On the Balance Sheet of Labor in the Kolkhozes,' in *Planned Economy* (1938), No. 12. See also Chapter III.b.

[9] Decree of 2 October 1940.

picture theaters opened. But when the growing savings of an individual member exceed the economic and legal possibilities of enlarging or improving his homestead farm and the family's need for durable consumers' goods, the surplus savings cannot, under present conditions, be productively utilized in the kolkhozes. Government policy forces their utilization in homesteads rather than in the kolkhoz—in the private not in the socialized sector of kolkhoz economy—and this utilization, too, is limited by law. When the kolkhozes were organized, it was hoped that 'in the kolkhozes the peasants will gradually grow out of their petty-bourgeois psychology, that their desire for private accumulation will disappear.' [10] In reality, this change takes place very slowly.

Thanks to the system of bonuses, shock workers and Stakhanovites receive increasingly large incomes. The average income of kolkhoz members is also growing, especially in kolkhozes producing industrial crops (cotton, flax, etc.). Deposits of members in savings banks are increasing. Members invest savings in homesteads, expand the output of private gardens, hives, and dairies. But the law imposes strict limitations on the possibilities of expanding the homestead. The problem of where the kolkhoz member may direct his savings remains unsolved; it will become even more acute with the increase of the average profitableness of kolkhozes.

Such a situation cannot continue indefinitely. Either the government must violate a fundamental principle of the Soviet economic system, permitting investment of savings in kolkhozes by members' purchase of supplementary dividend-paying shares, or it must regard the fact of increased savings in the hands of kolkhoz members as an index of kolkhoz economic consolidation and gradually re-organize them into State farms, transferring the workers to the wage system.

The chief reason why the government set up only a few State farms was the realization that, in the years of its industrialization

[10] *On the Agrarian Front* (1932), No. 1, pp. 1-2.

policy (since 1929), it would be unable to organize profitable State farms and assure farm labor a fixed wage.[11] But the financial and productive growth of the kolkhozes may prompt the government to revise organizational forms of agricultural production. Such may be the fate of the kolkhozes unless, under the influence of internal and external political conditions, they become free peasant co-operatives, independently solving the problems of utilization of income and of accumulation, both of the kolkhozes and of their members.

Older kolkhoz members, particularly formerly well-to-do peasants, who imbibed in their childhood the psychology of 'a small farm—but my own' and 'I am my own master,' found it hard to accept kolkhoz organization, and still have difficulty in adapting themselves. Their old dreams are deeply rooted. But the younger generation adjusts itself with relative ease to the new collective forms, especially since the kolkhozes have begun to assure them better living conditions. By 1940 more than half the population of working age had grown up under the Soviet regime, with no experience of any even relatively prosperous private economy. Hence the rapid social and psychological transformation of peasants into semi-workers, semi-participants in group enterprises with ever-diminishing psychological difficulties.

The average kolkhoz peasant has learned to admit the merits of the kolkhoz method. Were the government to reduce the share of income which it absorbs and allow more economic initiative to the kolkhozes, the peasantry might entirely abandon age-old dreams of independent private farms.

[11] Speech of Stalin, 26 March 1932.

XVII

Kolkhoz Officials: Selection and Status

IN the early kolkhoz days, the government had extreme difficulty in finding proper leaders. The poorest peasantry, on which it relied to carry out compulsory collectivization, was inexperienced and hence of little use for the administration of large-scale, complex enterprises. Those well-to-do peasants who joined kolkhozes—whether in good faith or to do disguised private farming or to utilize the kolkhoz for personal enrichment—were not trusted. The problem of kolkhoz administration was further complicated by the search for new organizational forms, the campaign for the liquidation of kulaks, and government demands for grain to feed urban workers.

Under these conditions, the government frequently felt compelled to send trusted city workers to act as rural leaders. In 1930 and 1931, 25,000 such workers were sent to rural areas as kolkhoz chairmen.[1] Sometimes, but not usually, 'for the sake of form,' their appointments were ratified by general membership meetings. Appointment of kolkhoz officers from above was the general practice. Appointment of city workers as chairmen and members of Managing Boards continued until 1938. According to official figures, more than 250,000 were appointed to permanent posts between 1928 and 1938.[2] In those years kolkhoz administrative staffs were composed chiefly of persons alien to rural life and without knowledge of local conditions or of the people among

[1] Stalin's address to the 17th Party Congress; *Problems of Leninism* (10th ed., Moscow, 1934), pp. 582-3.

[2] In 1932, several thousand workers were sent to serve in the Political Departments of Machine-Tractor Stations, i.e. to direct the kolkhozes.

whom they had to work. The local attitude was usually hostile. Naturally, the task of such appointed officials was extremely difficult.

The government tried to overcome these difficulties by embarking energetically and persistently on the 'training of kolkhoz cadres.' Wherever it found conditions favorable, the government advanced local people to the chairmanship, placing them under the vigilant supervision of the Political Departments. Since promulgation of the Statute of 1935, the economic consolidation of the kolkhoz system, and the gradual emergence of a supply of qualified local personnel, the government has instructed local Soviets and Party committees to 'safeguard democracy in the kolkhozes' and to advance local people by election. The government has confined itself, on the whole, to 'recommending' suitable candidates and to watching over them.

There has been no study of the social origins of kolkhoz administrators. It is, however, known that today the majority of chairmen are 'elected men,' trained in the kolkhozes and, frequently, in special courses for chairmen. Soviet novels delight in depicting kolkhoz chairmen risen from the status of paupers, shepherds, and landless peasants. But reports appearing in a Gosplan manual [3] do not bear out the picture; many administrators come from other rural strata.

From 1932 to 1938, the number of persons prepared and trained for kolkhoz work included 1,200,000 tractor and combine operators, 800,000 kolkhoz chairmen, members of Managing Boards, brigade leaders, and accountants; 150,000 agronomists and animal husbandmen; and more than 1,200,000 other agricultural specialists.[4] Education, to a considerable extent political but also vocational and cultural, is a constant labor. Gradually all administrative or specialized posts, including those of mechanics, tractor operators, brigade leaders, agronomists, livestock breeders, etc.,

[3] Gosplan, *Socialist Agriculture* (Moscow, 1939), pp. 103, 104.

[4] People's Commissariat for Agriculture, *Aid to the Kolkhoz Village* (Moscow, 1939), pp. 78-9.

are being filled by peasants 'promoted' from the ranks, often local kolkhoz peasants.

Among the negative aspects of kolkhoz administration was the turnover of personnel, especially chairmen, agronomists, tractor operators, and accountants. Higher, middle, and lower Soviet and Party authorities removed many, promoted others who proved their ability or enjoyed favor. Turnover became the veritable scourge of kolkhoz life. It hampered co-ordination and made impossible complicated projects requiring a period of several years for completion. It made it difficult to fix responsibility for results. As late as 1937, only 9.2 per cent of all chairmen, 6 per cent of all chairmen of Control Commissions, 8 per cent of farm managers, and 8.9 per cent of brigade leaders had held their posts for five years or more. Forty-six per cent of all kolkhoz chairmen, 47.1 per cent of all chairmen of Control Commissions, 43.6 per cent of managers of auxiliary farms (animals, chickens, bees, etc.), and 43.2 per cent of brigade leaders had been in their posts less than a year.[5] The turnover of elected officials was still going on in 1941.[6]

The government strove to fill the posts of chairmen with Communists. But in view of the small proportion of rural Communists, the percentage among chairmen, even during the years of compulsory collectivization, did not exceed 46. This percentage, moreover, has gradually diminished. In 1936 it was 30.2, in 1938 only 19. The percentage of Communists among specialists is even lower: at the beginning of 1938, there were 8.1 per cent of Communists among farm managers, 5.9 among livestock breeders, 6 among brigade leaders, and 14.2 among agronomists.[7]

The participation of women in kolkhoz administrations is considerable. At the end of 1937 women among brigade leaders constituted 19 per cent, squad leaders 66, farm managers 19, tractor

[5] Central Statistical Office, *The Kolkhozes in the Second Five Year Plan* (Moscow, 1939), pp. 60-66.

[6] *Party Construction* (1941), No. 10.

[7] *The Kolkhozes in the Second Five Year Plan*, pp. 67-84.

operators 7, agronomists 6. The percentage of women among kolkhoz chairmen is still rather low: in 1936 it was 1.8, in 1937, 2.6.

The age composition of the kolkhoz administrative staffs has fluctuated considerably. Today they contain many who have grown up in the period of the Revolution. Many officials have received general educations, many more broadened their horizons during service in the Red Army, which they remember as their 'university.' There is an especially large number of young people among technical personnel. The overwhelming majority of tractor and combine operators, electricians, agronomists, stock breeders, and brigade leaders are young people advanced to leading posts on the basis of work performed. Many rural youths finish the seventh year of school (i.e. urban elementary school) and return to the kolkhoz to be elected to leadership.

The considerably improved economic position of chairmen and other officials makes it easier to fill these posts with people of education and cultural background. A general study of kolkhozes made in 1939 showed that two-thirds of all chairmen had an elementary education, and 8 per cent partial or full secondary-school education.[8] There has been an increase in the number of chairmen who have had agricultural training or special courses. A detailed study in the Melitopol district indicates similar trends. Only one-fifth of all chairmen had previously been city workers or hired farmhands; 76 per cent of all chairmen stem from the villages of their kolkhoz, 7 per cent from neighboring villages; 60 per cent have had elementary education. In 1931 the percentage of Communists among chairmen was 50.2; in 1934, it was 43.1.[9]

A definite type of 'responsible worker' has evolved through the years. Whether or not he belongs to the Communist Party, he is usually conscious of ties with the Soviet system and the kolkhoz

[8] *Pravda*, 7 March 1940.

[9] A. Arina and I. Kotov, *Social-Economic Changes among the Peasantry of the Melitopol District* (Moscow, 1939), pp. 214-20.

order. This is owing partly to deliberate selection, partly to the influence of conditions of life and work. He has come to recognize that he is a part of the government, a carrier of Soviet policy. In recent years (say, 1938-40), with a decrease in arbitrary removals from posts and the economic stabilization of kolkhozes, such officials probably merge personal interests and plans with work. In the kolkhoz they find opportunities for satisfaction, a field for social activity.

During the early years, the attitude of rank-and-file members toward chairmen and members of Managing Boards was quite hostile, particularly when the latter were outsiders. They were regarded as government agents, instruments of coercive policies. In recent years, especially since the kolkhozes have, on the whole, proved their economic soundness and since economic conditions have improved for the mass of members, the ties between kolkhoz members and kolkhoz 'authorities' have grown stronger and relations have improved. There has come into existence a consciousness of a 'common cause,' and a greater understanding of the social usefulness of chairmen and brigade leaders.

Of course, there is a difference between the material standards of living of the chairman, the brigade leader, and the mass of members. The administrative staff lives better, has a higher and more assured income, better connections and protection in difficult moments. This standard of living is approached by rural Stakhanovites, 'shock-brigaders.' The average kolkhoz member still lives by hard labor and leads a meager, although gradually improving, existence. But during the years, the kolkhoz economic system has demonstrated its potentialities for providing a high standard of living to all its members.

Glossary of Russian Words and Phrases

Economsoviet (*Economicheskii Soviet*): Economic Soviet.
Glavk (*Glavnyi Komitet*): Main Industrial Board (or Committee); unit of State industrial administration just below the *Narkomat.*
Glavsbyt (*Glavnoye Sbytovoye Upravleniye*): Main Sales Board (of *Glavks* and *Narkomats*).
Glavsnab (*Glavnoye Upravleniye Snabzheniya*): Main Procurement Board (of *Narkomats*).
Gosplan (*Gosudarstvennaya Planovaya Komissiya*): State Planning Commission.
Khozraschet (*Khozyaistvennyi raschet*): Business accountability.
Khozyaistvennik: Economic official.
Kolkhoz (*Kollektivnoye khozyaistvo*): Collective farm.
Kombinat: Combine, complex type of plant producing wide range of goods based on single main raw material, with its by-products and waste.
Kulak: A wealthy peasant.
Narkom (*Narodnyi Komissar*): People's Commissar, the head of a People's Commissariat.
Narkomat (*Narodnyi Komissariat*): People's Commissariat, i.e. a government department in the sense of a Department of the United States federal government.
NEP (*Novaya Ekonomicheskaya Politika*): 'New Economic Policy' (1921-8), which temporarily restored free markets and some degree of free enterprise.
Obkom (*Oblastnoi Komitet*): Provincial (Communist) Party Committee.
Oblispolkom (*Oblastnoi Ispolnitel'nyi Komitet*): Executive Committee of a provincial Soviet, the highest organ of the provincial administration.
Politburo (*Politicheskoye Byuro*): Political Bureau (of the Central Committee of the Communist Party of the U.S.S.R.), the chief political authority in the Soviet Union.
Predpriyatiye: Enterprise (see *Plant* in Note on Terminology and Citations).
Pyatiletka: Five Year Plan.

Raiispolkom (*Raionnyi Ispolnitel'nyi Komitet*): Executive Committee of a district Soviet, the highest organ of the district administration.

Soviet: Council.

Sovkhoz (*Sovietskoye khozyaistvo*): A State-owned and State-managed farm, usually a model farm.

Sovnarkom (*Soviet Narodnykh Komisarov*): Council of People's Commissars; includes the heads of all the People's Commissariats.

Stakhanovetz (anglicized to Stakhanovite): A worker with special productive achievements to his credit, after Stakhanov, a record-breaking coal miner.

Tekhpromfinplan (*Tekhnichesko-promyshlenno-finansovyi plan*): An industrial plant's annual plan of technical development, production, and finances.

Toz (*Tovarishchestvo dlya sovmestnoi obrabotki zemli*): Society for joint land cultivation.

Yedino-natchaliye: One-man control (literally, single rule or authority; see *Control* in Note on Terminology and Citations).

Titles of Russian Periodicals

FOR Russian magazines, bulletins, and newspapers (with the exception of *Pravda* and *Izvestiya*) that have been cited in the text, the Russian titles are as follows. Except where otherwise noted, the place of publication is Moscow. For *Decisions* and *Laws and Ordinances* see Note on Terminology and Citations.

Bolshevik: *Bol'shevik,* magazine published fortnightly by the Central Committee of the Communist Party.

Bulletin for Economic and Financial Law: *Byulleten' Finansovogo i Khozyaistvennogo Zakonodatel'stva,* published by the People's Commissariat for Finance.

Bulletin of Soviet Russian Economics: *Byulleten' Ekonomicheskogo Kabineta Prof. S. N. Prokopovicha,* published in Prague until 1938; subsequently published in Geneva in English, as the Quarterly Bulletin of Soviet Russian Economics.

Economic Life: *Ekonomicheskaya Zhizn',* newspaper published by the People's Commissariat for Finance.

Economic Review: *Ekonomicheskoye Obozreniye,* magazine published monthly by the Supreme Economic Council.

Enterprise: *Predpriyatiye,* magazine published monthly by the newspaper *Pravda.*

Finances and Socialist Economy: *Finansy i Sotzialisticheskoye Khozyaistvo,* magazine published monthly by the People's Commissariat for Finance.

For Industrialization: *Za Industrializatziyu;* see Industry.

Industry: *Industriya,* newspaper published by the People's Commissariat for Heavy Industry (earlier title, *Za Industrializatziyu*).

Labor: *Trud,* newspaper published by the Central Trade Union Council.

Light Industry: *Legkaya Promyshlennost',* newspaper published by the People's Commissariat for Light Industry.

Machine-Building: *Mashinostroyeniye,* newspaper published by the three People's Commissariats for Machine-Building.

On the Agrarian Front: *Na Agrarnom Fronte,* magazine published monthly by the Agrarian Institute of the Communist Academy.

Party Construction: *Partiinoye Stroitel'stvo*, magazine published fortnightly by the Central Committee of the Communist Party.

The Plan: *Plan*, magazine published fortnightly by the Gosplan.

Planned Economy: *Planovoye Khozyaistvo*, magazine published monthly by the Gosplan.

Problems of the Economy: *Problemy Ekonomiki*, magazine published bimonthly, later monthly, by the Economic Institute of the Academy of Sciences.

Quarterly Bulletin of Soviet Russian Economics: see Bulletin of Soviet Russian Economics.

Socialist Agriculture: *Sotzialisticheskoye Zemledeliye*, newspaper published by the People's Commissariat for Agriculture.

Socialist Courier: *Sotzialisticheski Vestnik*, magazine published fortnightly by the Russian Social Democrats (1921-33 in Berlin, 1933-40 in Paris, since 1940 in New York).

Soviet Justice: *Sovietskaya Yustitziya*, magazine published fortnightly by the People's Commissariat for Justice.

The Stakhanovite: *Stakhanovetz*, magazine published monthly by the Central Trade Union Council.

Steel: *Stal'*, magazine published monthly in Kharkov by the Steel Glavk, later by the People's Commissariat for Ferrous Metallurgy.

Index